CATECHESIS
AND
MYSTAGOGY
INFANT BAPTISM

Paul Covino

Catherine Dooley

Angie Fagarason

Timothy Fitzgerald

Linda Gaupin

James Moudry

James Musemeci

Jane Marie Osterholt

David Philippart

Patricia Hawkins Vaillancourt

Mary Alice Roth

Deanne Tumpich

Liturgy Training Publications

PUBLISHING

D1118404

Acknowledgments

Excerpts from the English translation of the *Rite of Baptism for Children* © 1969, International Committee on English in the Liturgy, Inc. (ICEL); excerpts from the English translation of the *Rite of Christian Initiation of Adults* © 1985, ICEL; excerpts from *The Liturgical Psalter* © 1994, 1995, ICEL. All rights reserved.

Excerpts from *Catholic Household Blessings and Prayers* © 1988, United States Catholic Conference, Inc. All rights reserved.

Project coordinator: Robert Piercy
Editor: Victoria M. Tufano
Production editor: Kathy Luty
Designer: Jill Smith
Production artist: Karen Mitchell
Original cover photo: Richard Meats/Tony Stone Images

This book was set in New Century Schoolbook and Charme type and printed by Quebecor Printing Book Group.

Printed in the United States of America.

Copublished with Tabor Publishing Company, 200 East Bethany Drive, Allen TX 75002; 214-390-6300; FAX 214-727-9589

Library of Congress Cataloging-in-Publications Data
Catechesis and mystagogia: infant baptism / Paul Covino . . . [et al.].
    p.   cm.
   Includes bibliographical references.
   ISBN 1-56854-108-2
    1. Infant baptism. 2. Baptism — Catholic Church. 3. Catholic Church — Doctrines. 4. Cathechetics — Catholic Church. 5. Mystagogy — Catholic Church.
I. Covino, Paul.
BV813.2.C37   1996
264'.020812 — dc20

                                           96-5498
                                           CIP

Contents

The Reform of Christian Initiation: An Introduction

James Moudry

Prior to the Second Vatican Council's reforms of Christian initiation, the Catholic Church's experience of baptism was pretty much defined by the baptism of infants. There were the occasional adult converts who became Catholic through a process carried on mysteriously between themselves and the parish priest, but that process remained unknown to the average Catholic parishioner. It was the baptism of infants that dominated the meaning of baptism for Catholics. Even though it was usually a privately celebrated liturgy, a large percentage of Catholics witnessed the baptism of a baby at some point in their lives.

With the promulgation of the *Rite of Christian Initiation of Adults* (1972) and its pastoral implementation in the years since, the picture has changed dramatically. Though far from uniformly accepted, understood and implemented, the adult initiation ministry nonetheless has been a pastoral experience of great power in the church. Its promise continues. It has galvanized parish energy and resources, and it has changed the face of Christian initiation in the Catholic Church. Based as it is on a New Testament and early church pattern of evangelization and catechesis aimed at conversion and learning how to live the Christian life, it has caused the church to rethink the relationship between the experience of conversion and the sacraments of initiation. Initiation is no longer about "getting the sacraments" so much as it is about learning to live as disciples of Jesus and members of his community, dedicated to Jesus' dream for the world, which in the gospels is called the kingdom of God. The initiation sacraments are the communal rituals which celebrate that conversion-discipleship reality, giving public, ecclesial shape to God's embrace of the new believer.

The reform of adult initiation in the Roman Catholic Church has swept before it all initiation practice. Its ritual structure and catechetical process have been put forward by some commentators as the norm (the standard according to which a thing is done) for baptism. From this perspective infant baptism is an "abnormality," although a benign one that is clearly legitimate in certain circumstances.[1] Such a perspective has led some to question the appropriateness of infant baptism altogether and it has led others to legitimately ask what we are to think of infant baptism in light of the reform of adult initiation. It would be unfortunate if an adversarial relationship were to emerge between the practices of adult and infant initiation; I do not think this is the intent of those who promote the values of the reform of adult initiation, nor do I think that the reform has to relegate infant baptism to the status of a "poor cousin," a source of embarrassment. Christian initiation is an experience of church life so rich that no single model or paradigm will exhaust it.

Clearly, the reform of adult initiation has greatly enriched the church's practice of adult baptism. At the same time, the church also has renewed the practice of infant baptism in the form of the *Rite of Baptism for Children,* promulgated in 1969. Many of its finest features were echoed in the adult rite, which appeared three years later.

The *Rite of Baptism for Children* and the *Rite of Christian Initiation of Adults* belong to the same church and together are intended to represent a coherent and consistent picture of initiation. Unbaptized infants and adults represent two different pastoral challenges, both of which can disclose to the church the richness of the ways God interacts with the human condition. Therefore, far from being seen as a problem to be grappled with, infant initiation can be seen as "an opportunity to be grasped."[2]

This book, *Catechesis and Mystagogy: Infant Baptism,* sets out to grasp this opportunity. Simply in terms of the number of people being baptized, infant baptism outweighs adult initiation. It remains, therefore, a significant pastoral opportunity in church life that ought not to be neglected. It is time to look again at the practice of infant baptism in light of the entire reform of Christian initiation. This introduction will explore the vision of initiation set forth in the two rites to see how they can enrich each other in the understanding and practice of baptism. The rest of the book will make pastoral applications for parish life.

3

The Rite of Christian Initiation of Adults

We begin by recalling the principal elements of the vision of adult initiation according to the *Rite of Christian Initiation of Adults.*

1. *Initiation is a gradual process.* The rite compares it to a journey — a spiritual and holistic journey.

2. *The community itself is the principal companion for those on the journey, and it ministers with them.* As a result of the demands of accompanying those to be initiated, the community itself is renewed in its own identity, life and purpose. The particular ministries named in the rite are intended to focus the community's ministry, not to stand as surrogate for it.

3. *At the heart of the journey is ritual.* Strategically located at certain stages are major liturgical celebrations that mark and shape

the initiation process. Ritual prayer saturates the entire catechetical experience.

4. *Consequently, the reform calls for a unique catechetical process in which ritual experience becomes the anchor and foundation for catechesis.* The liturgies of the rite set the agenda for catechetical formation. The whole process is driven by the liturgy.

5. *The initiation journey is connected to the celebration of the liturgical feasts and seasons.* The word of God proclaimed from the lectionary within the celebration of the church's liturgy guides the people through the liturgical year. The centerpiece of the journey is the paschal season in which word, sacrament and sacred time come together to express and support the meaning of initiation.

6. *The goal of the journey is faith in Jesus Christ and life in the community.* The church's initiation structures exist to support and gently guide the mysterious and powerful work of conversion, which the Spirit of God does in the life of the person. The faith life of the community models for the convert the distinctive shape of her or his conversion, including its consequences for mission and ministry. The hoped-for outcome of Christian initiation extends beyond the reception of sacraments to a life of genuine discipleship.

4

Enrichment of Infant Baptism

Can the vision of Christian initiation found in the adult rite contribute to the understanding and practice of infant baptism? Yes. Some of the emphases from the adult rite can reinforce what the *Rite of Baptism for Children* already calls for. Without claiming to be exhaustive, the following points can easily be drawn.

1. *The emphasis on conversion that marks the adult rite underlines the necessity of a living faith as the context for the celebration of infant baptism.* Of course, the church has always argued against "indiscriminate" infant baptism, that is, the baptism of a child where there is no reasonable expectation that the child will be supported in the practice of the faith. But the adult rite reinforces

the need for the community to work with parents and godparents, supporting them in their own practice of the faith, which is to be the matrix for the child's developing faith.

2. *The image of initiation as a journey that extends over time in order to come to the right moment for baptism can remind us not to rush the baptism of infants.* This relates to the previous point that the faith context, which takes time to emerge, must be present.

3. *The goal of initiation is not to "get the sacrament" but to make disciples.* If the pastoral practice of infant baptism takes that goal seriously, it will look carefully to the pre- and postbaptismal moments of the initiation process. Often overlooked in our practice is post-ritual catechesis that will support the parents in their own faith formation and in their care for the religious formation of their children.

Developmental psychology tells us that attitudes, values and behavior patterns are set for life in the first five years of childhood. Yet many parish communities do not make efforts to support parents of young children in their faith formation responsibilities. The consequences of this are often startling when those same parents return with their children for grade school and/or first communion.

4. *If liturgy is central to the initiation of Christians, it can play a central role in the catechesis of parents presenting infant children for baptism.* Working creatively with the baptismal rite itself—its scripture, symbols and environment—forms faith gently and respectfully. Helping parents and godparents connect their evolving life stories with the symbols of baptism is always fresh, never boring. It offers an opportunity for spiritual deepening.

5. *No less than with adults, the baptism of infants is intimately connected with the liturgical year.* The meaning of the sacrament can be fully expressed only in the context of the paschal season. As with the adult rite, the time for celebrating infant baptism is not a matter of indifference.

5

6. *Because it is the Holy Spirit who directs people's conversion, it is always a sacred moment when parents request baptism for their children.* Regardless of the parents' personal situation, the request deserves to be honored and respected. The movement of the Spirit and the calendar of parish programs do not always mesh. It behooves us to try to be on the side of the Spirit.

Rite of Baptism for Children

As important as the reform of the adult rite for Christian initiation is, there are lessons to be learned from the *Rite of Baptism for Children*. Many of these lessons are in the form of broad principles that invite reflection on the pastoral practice of infant baptism. The chapters in this book will address some of those pastoral implications. In some cases, the perspective offered by the rite for children challenges us to reflect on the whole of the church's initiation ministry, including the initiation of adults.

Early church tradition teaches us that Christians are "made, not born." Christian initiation is an action of regeneration. The gospel understanding of conversion requires a "turning from" and a "turning toward," a leaving behind of what was in order to embrace what will be; the adult rite's emphasis on conversion embodies this understanding. Because Christian initiation is characterized by such discontinuity, the dominance in the adult rite of the paschal model of death-resurrection fits well.

The moment of infant baptism celebrates a graced action of God, with respect to the child, that is definitive for the child's situation. But for infants born into a Christian family, the family itself is the first embodiment of grace. The Catholic Church's understanding of the sacrament of matrimony is that it is a sign and cause of grace that makes the family a domestic church, a communion of life in Christ. The family participates in the mystery of the church, the sacrament of Christ. Baptism celebrates the faith life of the church, and, in the case of infant baptism, that faith finds its first expression in the domestic church.

Although baptism is an act of regeneration, in the case of a child of a believing household, there is an immediate and sacred prior fact — namely, human generation itself. The child of such a graced sacramental union is born into a "little church." The sacramental encounter at the baptismal font is not the first meeting between God and the child. In other words, while it remains true that Christians are "made, not born," in the case of an infant child of a Christian marriage, the "making" begins with the act of generation. Rather than the discontinuity that characterizes the adult pattern of initiation, the continuity between the "before" and "after" status of the infant seems more obvious. (Is not the fact of belonging to this domestic church frequently invoked to allay the fears of parents about the fate of an infant who dies without baptism?)

What might this continuity of the infant's situation suggest for pastoral practice? The image of initiation as journey, emphasized in the adult rite, certainly applies. But more emphatic ought to be the recognition of the sacredness of the entire birth event: the sexual act of generation; pregnancy; the birth of the child; the first holding of the infant by parents, siblings and grandparents; the naming; the first feeding of the child and the beginning of parental care; bringing the child home (when the birth has occurred elsewhere); "showing" the child to relatives, friends and neighbors. These things and more are the sacred stuff of human generation, and all of this is the epiphany of the domestic church, the enfleshing of the Divine Spirit! It is on the surface of this already sacred domestic church experience that there erupts the larger church's rite of infant baptism. The rite celebrates what God is already doing in the life of this family and infant, enfolding it in a new and public way, in a definitive altering of the infant's status.

A continuing danger in church ministry is to make faith formation too "churchy" too soon. This is residue from our "two-story universe" mentality, which fails to recognize sufficiently the

7

sacredness of ordinary life experiences. It is understandable that a church with celibate male leadership will struggle to appreciate the holiness of marriage, sexuality, birth and the intimate particulars of family life. One of the benefits of expanding faith-formation ministries to include lay people, especially married lay people, ought to be greater recognition of the already sacred character of family life in pastoral catechesis.

Images of Christian Initiation

The richness of the initiation experience of the Christian community is expressed in the images of baptism found in the tradition. Here again, infant baptism is instructive. As already mentioned, the emphasis of adult initiation is on the journey of conversion that comes to faith in Christ, a faith that is sealed in the initiation sacraments and flowers in discipleship. It is a journey of discontinuity, of dying to sin and rising to new life. The paschal image of Christ's death and resurrection, into which the believer is spliced, is the glue that holds the parts of initiation together and requires its celebration at the paschal feast.

As rich as the paschal image is, if it were the sole image for interpreting the meaning of baptism it would make understanding infant baptism difficult. The radical discontinuity that the paschal journey implies is not easily imagined in the situation of infants born into Christian households. Thankfully, there are other New Testament images of baptism. A prominent one is the baptism of the Lord at the Jordan River. It provides motifs for baptism such as adoption, divinization, holiness, glory, power and rebirth — all images that are more compatible with infant baptism.[3] We would do well to keep all of the images in fruitful tension with one another.

Suitable though it may be for adult initiation, the imagery of the paschal mystery does not exhaust baptism's meaning, nor is it always the most pastorally effective. Death-resurrection is a straight-line image, masculine in its overtones. When liturgists and theologians explore patterns of initiation in primitive cultures for help in understanding Christian initiation, they frequently are led to the paradigm offered by Arnold Van Gennep at the beginning of this century. Van Gennep sees initiation in three moments: separation, liminality and reaggregation. As helpful as that paradigm might be for deepening our understanding of the paschal mystery as *transitus,* more recent research has shown that most of those tribal initiation rites pertained to the initiation of males — the initiation of females followed a quite different path.

There are pastoral risks in restricting baptismal imagery. Imaging baptism as birth, font as womb, or initiation as divine adoption, carries other, more feminine, connotations. All of these belong to the tradition; and, thankfully, the practice of infant baptism helps us not to lose sight of them.

9

Infant Baptism and the Renewal of the Church

One of the more dramatic and important changes in the reform of infant baptism is that the rite no longer asks the community, the parents and godparents to speak for the child but for themselves. The essays in this book richly make this point. The adults speak their own renunciation of sin, their own profession of faith and their commitment to the spiritual care of the infant. This emphasis echoes a key perspective of the entire reform of Christian initiation, namely, that initiation is the occasion for the renewal of the church itself. Initiation is not something done to others. Rather, it is an invitation to others to join in living the gospel values of the reign of God which the community promises to live right now.

In the baptismal ritual, the parents commit themselves to being church for their child — a domestic church where faith and discipleship are learned while living together as a family. The affirmative response to the question "Do you promise to raise your child in the practice of the faith?" represents a public commitment of the highest order. The church is being born again!

A major challenge in the reform of adult initiation has been how to involve the community in the initiation ministry that is properly theirs. Perhaps because in infant baptism the one being initiated is so obviously helpless, the promise of the community to be there for the child seems more real. Adult converts can more easily fend for themselves, or so it appears. Supported by a catechumenal team, they have made a lengthy journey climaxing in a public statement of personal conversion. The community can watch and admire that from a distance—not so when the object of the community's promise of care is the dependent infant. But what is the responsibility of the community toward this child? How is that responsibility lived out in the parish? These questions will be addressed in this book.

Baptism, an Act of Salvation

The practice of baptizing infants raises for the church a foundational issue in the divine economy of salvation. In the long history of Christian initiation, there have been those who have challenged the legitimacy of infant baptism, insisting that only a believer's baptism is faithful to the New Testament teaching of justification by faith.

The attractiveness and power of a believer's baptism is undeniable. We need only think of the impact of the experience of the catechumenate in our parishes. To hear adults give public testimony to their faith conversion, to watch them meet death to sin in the waters of the font, to see them rise and be sealed with the fragrance of Christ's Spirit and come to the eucharistic table of discipleship—all of that stirs the hearts and strengthens the resolve of parishioners.

What can be obscured (but not negated) in that dramatic enactment, though, is that the wonder of personal conversion is the consequence of the prior action of God. Our dramatic and rich initiation structures do not produce salvation. God's word-deed is always prior and sufficient. In short, we do not identify the biblical doctrine of justification by faith with a conscious act of adult commitment to Christ and then make that the prerequisite for salvation and church membership. When we fall into that mode of thinking, we are, in effect, saying that God's gracious initiative is ineffective until we ratify it personally. Have we not sometimes used that line of thinking to explain the meaning of the sacrament of confirmation when it is separated from baptism and delayed until the teen years?

Infant baptism has stood through the centuries to remind us of the priority and sufficiency of God's gracious action toward us, regardless of our ability to respond. Infants do nothing at their baptism — they make no promises, no profession of faith. As mentioned earlier, it is the community, especially the parents, who makes the professions and declarations that represent their own beliefs and their own commitment to the child's care. Infant initiation is an eloquent testimony to our belief in God's saving initiative and graciousness on our behalf. In today's personalist and individualist climate, wherein we measure the success of our liturgies (adult initiation liturgies included) by how personally meaningful they are and how much we "get out of them," the baptizing of infants serves as an important and necessary reminder of what we believe about God's action in liturgical events.

11

Infant Baptism, Church and Mission

Infant baptism presents an opportunity to reflect more deeply on the meaning of family in a renewed understanding of church. Mark Searle has observed that

> The clerical-monastic church sees itself as liminal to the world, but it sees the Christian family as peripheral to itself and thus abandons it to the realm of the secular. This may have worked while church and society were coextensive, but in today's society it is at least arguable that the liminality characteristic of the kingdom of God is no longer localized in the church as denominational institution . . . but in the Christian family. . . . It is in the

family, or in clusters of families, that genuinely countercultural issues . . . are capable of being addressed. But for
this we need a theology of family.[4]

If the practice of infant baptism can help strengthen the theology
and experience of family life, it will contribute to the ultimate
reason for a renewed initiation ministry in the church. The goal of
initiation is the making of disciples who will contribute to the
transformation of our society so that it mirrors more faithfully God's
dream for the world. In our society, as Searle observed, it is the
family that struggles with countercultural issues, especially in the
raising of children. Infant baptism is a pastoral opportunity to be
grasped for the sake of clarifying and supporting the role of the
domestic church in the work of making present the kingdom of God
in the world.

What to Expect in This Book

This and other recent books on infant baptism[5] are not going over
old ground. Rather, they are invitations to seize in new and creative
ways the pastoral opportunity presented by the birth of infants.
This invitation goes out to the whole parish community, but especially to parish ministers, to work and dream together. The
fragmentation and compartmentalizing of pastoral ministry will
not renew the church.

 This book opens with a statement of principles about the
liturgical and sacramental life of the church. Read these principles
more than once. If possible, engage others in conversation about
their implications for parish practice. That examination of
principles is followed by Paul Covino's brief overview of infant
baptism ("our roots"), and his analysis of the *Rite of Baptism for
Children*, which includes catechetical reflections ("our rites") and a
listing of pertinent resource material.

 The following two chapters deal with liturgy and catechesis.
Chapter 2, by Jane Marie Osterholt, is a welcome contribution to a

topic needing clarity—method. Osterholt models a catechetical method that starts with the ritual elements of infant baptism and invites parents, godparents and the community to explore what these elements say about the meaning of baptism and everyday life. To aid in the catechesis of the assembly, Osterholt has prepared a series of bulletin inserts based on the material in that chapter; those inserts can be found on pages 106–109 and may be copied for use by purchasers of this book. Chapter 3, by Patricia Hawkins Vaillancourt, takes us deeper into catechesis, catechetical content and process. She writes sensitively about the unique situation that occurs when a child is born into a family. Her observations on family life have a strong feel of reality about them. Her chapter includes suggestions for organizing catechetical sessions and for developing a catechetical process respectful of adults.

A significant development stemming from liturgical reform has been the recognition that the time for celebrating a liturgy can be an important factor in understanding its meaning. Sacramental celebrations and liturgical time are connected. Linda Gaupin carefully analyzes the church's directives that affect the time for the celebration of infant baptism. What was once thought to be of little import is now acknowledged as significant. The implications for pastoral practice are important.

Angie Fagarason, Mary Alice Roth and Deanne Tumpich offer their parish's experience of taking seriously the celebration of infant baptism, even when it takes place outside the Sunday eucharist. Because it is an act of the entire parish community, the parish provides a full complement of ministers for the celebration.

David Philippart demonstrates again the rich formation in faith that can happen when the symbols of the liturgical action are given careful attention. His article is filled with helpful, practical suggestions for a good celebration. In the following chapter, Philippart provides a model of how one might preach on the rites and symbols of baptism.

13

Readers looking for an example of a program of pastoral care surrounding the baptism of infants will find it in the essay by James Musumeci. It includes detailed explanations of the program, the expectations of the participants, and even sample letters. In addition, suggestions for developing a program appropriate for other pastoral situations are offered.

In the final chapter, "Mystagogy: Ministry to Parents," Catherine Dooley examines the implications of the profession of faith and the commitment made by the parents during the baptism of their child and applies them to the postbaptismal period. She notes that the early years of childhood are crucial for the child's religious development but that very little pastoral attention has been given to the support of parents. She offers some concrete suggestions for post-ritual catechesis.

In addition to the bulletin inserts mentioned previously, the appendix of this book includes the study guide that was prepared for use with the video *New Life: A Parish Celebrates Infant Baptism*, a joint project of Liturgy Training Publications (LTP) and Tabor Publishing. This video shows how one parish regularly baptizes infants during the Sunday eucharist. It is an excellent companion to this book. The study guide, by Timothy Fitzgerald, offers many questions for reflection that may be helpful to ponder even without seeing the video.

14

Conclusion

The essays in this book help us grasp the pastoral opportunity presented by infant baptism. It is a continuing source of wonder how the most familiar, taken for granted, unchallenged things in our faith tradition, when juxtaposed with insights coming from another quarter, can become sources of genuine renewal for the church. Today, infant baptism is such a thing. Infused with insights from the reform of adult initiation, from the budding theology of family as domestic church, from the new relationships between liturgy and catechesis, from the postconciliar theology of church and sacraments, and from a new appreciation of the place of the child in the divine plan for salvation, the practice of infant baptism opens up new possibilities for the renewal of the church. Let us heed the word of God:

> Taking a child, Jesus placed it in their midst. (Mark 9:36)
>
> Let the children come to me . . . for the kingdom of God belongs to such as these. (Mark 10:14)
>
> Then the wolf shall be a guest of the lamb,
> and the leopard shall lie down with the kid;
> the calf and the young lion shall browse together,
> with a little child to guide them. (Isaiah 11:6)

Endnotes

1. Aidan Kavanagh, *The Shape of Baptism* (New York: Pueblo Publishing Company, 1978), 107–10.

2. Mark Searle, *Alternative Futures for Worship,* vol. 2: *Baptism and Confirmation* (Collegeville: The Liturgical Press, 1987), 50.

3. For the development of the adoption image, see Kurt Stasiak, "Infant Baptism Reclaimed: Forgotten Truths About Infant Baptism," *Living Light,* 31 (spring 1995): 36–46.

4. "Response: The RCIA and Infant Baptism," *Worship* 56 (1982): 331.

5. See Timothy Fitzgerald, *Infant Baptism: A Parish Celebration* (Chicago: Liturgy Training Publications, 1994).

Overview of Principles
for the Sacramental Life
of a Parish

T his book is a compilation of the words and experiences of many authors, but it represents a shared point of view. This point of view is scriptural, traditional and justice-oriented. In short, it is deeply Catholic. Yet it took many discussions among several people who represent the disciplines of liturgy and catechesis in the United States to arrive at a specific expression of this point of view.

These discussions took place as two publishing companies — Tabor Publishing of Allen, Texas, a publisher of catechetical materials, and Liturgy Training Publications, the publishing arm of the Office for Divine Worship of the Archdiocese of Chicago — began to explore the possibility of working together to produce materials on the sacraments. These discussions included, at various times, Eileen Anderson, Paul Covino, Ralph Fletcher, Catherine Dooley, OP, Timothy Fitzgerald, Gabe Huck, Jane Marie Osterholt, SP, Robert Piercy, Jo Rotunno and John Wright. As a common vision began to emerge, it was expressed in ten principles to which everyone involved could give assent. These principles were then given to those who would work on this book and other projects as a guideline.

The ten principles, listed here, present a vision not only for catechesis and mystagogy regarding infant baptism and all the sacraments but also for all of parish life. In the end, these principles are more important than any of the particulars about infant baptism presented in this book. If each parish — staff, ministers, people — wrestled with these principles and tried to live by them, preparing for and drawing meaning from infant baptism and all of the church's sacramental acts would, the authors believe, be an integral part of the way we are as church.

The authors invite you and those with whom you work in parish ministry to ponder, discuss and argue about these principles, and maybe even add to them. To assist in this endeavor, Liturgy Training Publications and Tabor Publishing have put together a workbook based on these principles, *A Common Sense for Parish Life*. Use it if it helps, but however you do it, spend some time with these principles. Your parish's life is worth it.

17

The Principles

1. We believe that creation, humanity and human deeds always hold and reveal the presence of God. This sacramental stance is the foundation of our way of living in the world.

2. The life of a parish is manifest in
   - attending to God's word, interceding, praising and giving thanks to God at the Sunday eucharist and in prayer and ritual of many kinds (worship);
   - forming members — young and old, new and veteran — through many ways of teaching (catechesis);
   - building up the body of Christ, the church (community);
   - witnessing to justice and caring for all those in need (service).

3. Scripture is integral to liturgy and to every aspect of parish life.

4. Sacramental life and celebration flourish when all parish ministers, especially those responsible for catechesis and liturgy, work together and share a vision.

5. Catechesis for all ages takes place within the community in a great variety of settings. In catechesis we are challenged and enabled to ponder, to question and to draw one another on in understanding of and zeal for the gospel.

6. Liturgy and catechesis bring the "power of the gospel into the very heart of culture and cultures."

7. Sunday eucharist is the central action of parish life. It has a vital relationship to all parish activities, especially to the daily lives of all the baptized.

8. The sacraments are the normal actions and celebrations of the assembly, which is all the baptized persons of a parish. The parish itself, then, is the primary symbol because it is the church, the body of Christ, that transacts the sacraments. We believe and we act, not as individuals but as the church, and even as this church, this parish.

9. The church's year organizes the sacramental work of the parish.

10. The celebration of the liturgy, supported by lifelong study, leads to the doing of justice.

Our Roots and Our Rites

Paul Covino

Every worker needs proper tools. For sacramental ministers, those tools are many: a knowledge of the people with whom they work, listening skills, compassion and wisdom, to name but a few. This chapter will provide the foundations for two other essential tools for those who minister to households preparing for the baptism of an infant: a knowledge of the scriptural and historical roots of the sacraments, and a knowledge of the rites of baptism.

Our Roots: The Background to Baptism

Baptism has been part of the church since the earliest days of Christianity. The letters of Saint Paul in the New Testament speak of baptism as the way Christians take part in Christ's death and resurrection:

> Do you not know that all of us who have been baptized into Christ Jesus were baptized into his death? Therefore we have been buried with him by baptism into death, so that, just as Christ was raised from the dead by the glory of the Father, so we too might walk in newness of life. (Romans 6:3–4)

The readings that we hear during the Easter season from the Acts of the Apostles recount the baptism of individuals, families, households and even large crowds of people in the early days of the church. Although children are not specifically mentioned, the Catholic Church has always taught that they were among these first groups to be baptized (*Rite of Baptism for Children,* 2).

The first clear reference to the baptism of children comes from a document known as the *Apostolic Tradition of Hippolytus,* written about the year 215. Describing an early third-century Easter Vigil in Rome, Hippolytus writes,

> And they shall baptize the little children first. And if they can answer for themselves, let them answer. But if they cannot, let their parents answer or someone from their family. (E. C. Whitaker, *Documents of the Baptismal Liturgy,* London: SPCK, 1960, p. 5)

The rite of baptism that developed in the early church was suited for adults. Like our current *Rite of Christian Initiation of Adults* (RCIA), it was designed to lead an adult through the process of conversion, that is, of turning from a past way of life to take on the Christian way of life. It included a lengthy period of formation as well as blessings and liturgies celebrated with the local Christian community. The rite reached its high point at the Easter Vigil in the celebration of the sacraments of initiation: baptism, confirmation and eucharist.

When children were presented for baptism, a condensed version of this rite was celebrated. The formation that *led up to* initiation for adults *came after* baptism in the case of children. Over the course of the centuries, baptism came to be celebrated shortly after the birth of a child, whereas confirmation and eucharist were delayed until the child was involved in catechesis. In the twentieth century, confirmation has been shifted more and more to the preteen and teenage years. Even though infant baptism became much more common than adult baptism, the rite celebrated when a child was baptized continued to be the condensed version of adult baptism.

In 1963, the Second Vatican Council directed that "the rite for the baptism of infants is to be revised and it should be suited to the fact that those to be baptized are infants" (*Constitution on the Sacred Liturgy* [CSL], 67). In 1969, Pope Paul VI issued the *Rite of Baptism for Children* (RBC), the church's first rite of baptism designed for infants and young children.

Our Rites: The Rite of Baptism for Children

The *Rite of Baptism for Children* has two introductions and seven chapters. The first introduction concerns Christian initiation in general and applies to the *Rite of Christian Initiation of Adults* and the *Rite of Confirmation* as well as to infant baptism. The second introduction is specifically for infant baptism. The first five chapters provide the texts and liturgical guidelines for the baptism of several children (chapter 1), one child (chapter 2) and a large number of children (chapter 3), as well as for baptism administered by a catechist when no priest or deacon is available (chapter 4) and baptism in danger of death when no priest or deacon is available (chapter 5). Chapter 6 provides a rite for bringing a baptized child to the church when the child was baptized outside of church because of the danger of death or some other serious reason. Chapter 7 contains various scripture and prayer texts for the celebration of baptism.

The *Rite of Baptism for Children* is the church's vision of how a parish is called to celebrate the baptism of infants and young children. It is also a primary source for the church's teaching about this sacrament. The text of this rite is the common starting point for all who are involved in leading the parish's baptismal ministry: priests, deacons, catechists, liturgy committees, pastoral musicians, baptismal teams. The rite provides the unifying vision for the collaboration among these various parish ministers. Rereading the rite every few years is a good exercise for seeing how well the parish is living out the church's vision of baptism.

21

Who?

The Second Vatican Council taught that "liturgical services are not private functions, but are celebrations belonging to the church" (CSL, 26). The baptism of an infant or young child concerns not only the child, but also the parents, the godparents, and the larger community of the parish and the whole church. The *Rite of Baptism for Children* gives a central role to the parents and the larger community, and a secondary role to the godparents. We can see this in the text of the rite itself. Prior to 1969, the questions in the rite were addressed to the child, and the godparents supplied the response; in the current rite, the prayers and other texts of the rite are primarily addressed to the parents, who profess their own faith and the faith of the church.

The rite outlines the ways in which the parents fulfill their role during the baptismal liturgy:

> a) they publicly ask that the child be baptized; b) they sign their child with the sign of the cross after the celebrant; c) they renounce Satan and make their profession of faith; d) they . . . carry the child to the font; e) they hold the lighted candle; f) they are blessed with the special prayers for the mothers and fathers. (RBC, 5.3)

The rite also stresses the parents' primary role in the Christian formation of the child:

> After baptism it is the responsibility of the parents . . . to enable the child to know God, whose adopted child it has become, to receive confirmation, and to participate in the holy eucharist. (RBC, 5.5)

The larger church, made present in the local parish community, also has an important role in the celebration of baptism and in the Christian formation of children:

> Before and after the celebration of the sacrament, the child has a right to the love and help of the community. During the rite, in addition to the ways of congregational participation . . . the community exercises its duty when it expresses its assent together with the celebrant after the profession of faith by the parents and godparents. In this way it is clear that the faith in which the children are

baptized is not the private possession of the individual
family but is the common treasure of the whole church of
Christ. (RBC, 4)

To make the community's role clear, the rite states a clear
preference for celebrating baptism "in the presence of the faithful"
(RBC, 32) and "even during Mass, so that the entire community may
be present" (RBC, 9).

Godparents have an important part in the baptism of infants
and young children, although the *Rite of Baptism for Children*
makes it clear that "because of the natural relationships, parents
have a more important ministry and role in the baptism of infants
than the godparents" (RBC, 5). The role of the godparents is to
support the parents, as we see from the question that is addressed
to them at the beginning of the rite: "Are you ready to help these
parents in their duty as Christian mothers and fathers?" (RBC, 40).

23

What?

As Catholics, we believe that the words and actions of our
sacraments "nourish, strengthen and express" faith (CSL, 59). In the
Rite of Baptism for Children, the texts and symbolic actions of the
rite embody and express the church's faith concerning baptism.
Baptismal catechesis enables us to reflect on the mysteries of the
faith as they are celebrated in the rite. It is important, therefore, to
pay attention to how well the parish celebrates baptism. Consider
the catechesis that arises from the following symbols of the rite:

- The preferred communal setting for baptism reflects the
  corporate nature of Christian faith.

- The signing of the children with the cross at the beginning
  of the rite signals the central place of the cross and selfless
  service in the life of Christians.

- The water connects the newly baptized child to God's use of
  water throughout salvation history and, especially, to
  Christ's death and resurrection.

- The anointing with chrism is a sign of being joined to the body of Christ, who "was anointed priest, prophet, and king" (RBC, 62).

- The clothing with the baptismal garment reflects the child's Christian dignity as a new creation in Christ.

- The lighted candle embodies the light of Christ which enlightens the newly baptized child and which, we pray, may "be kept burning brightly" (RBC, 64) in the way the child lives.

Catechesis and the parish's understanding of baptism are enhanced when these symbolic actions are celebrated well. Therefore, the *Rite of Baptism for Children* challenges parishes to make the fullest possible use of the symbols of baptism. For example, the rite encourages baptism by immersion because it "is more suitable as a symbol of participation in the death and resurrection of Christ" (*General Introduction,* 22). The rite also directs parents to clothe their children in the baptismal garments after the baptism in water and the anointing with chrism as a sign that they "have become a new creation and have clothed [themselves] in Christ" (RBC, 63). The meaning of this rite is, in fact, obscured when the children are brought to the church already wearing the baptismal garments. It is well worth the effort to build a parish tradition of baptismal liturgies that are celebrated in their full symbolic richness. Several articles in this book, especially David Philippart's "Grace through Sacramental Signs" (chapter 6), discuss further the need to be attentive to the full use of symbols.

When?

The issue of when to celebrate baptism also has catechetical implications. *The Rite of Baptism for Children* recommends certain occasions for the celebration of baptism in order to "bring out the paschal character of baptism" (RBC, 9). The Easter Vigil and Sundays are suggested as appropriate because these are when "the church commemorates the Lord's resurrection" (RBC, 9). The rite

24

goes on to say that baptism "should be conferred in a communal celebration for all the recently born children and in the presence of the faithful" (RBC, 32) and that it "may be celebrated even during Mass, so that the entire community may be present and the necessary relationship between baptism and eucharist may be clearly seen" (RBC, 9). See Linda Gaupin's article in this book, "When to Celebrate Baptism" (chapter 4), for a fuller discussion of this point.

Other Pertinent Resources

In this chapter, we have focused on the *Rite of Baptism for Children* as the common starting point for all who are involved in the parish's baptismal ministry. There are several other resources that complement the ritual text:

The *Catechism of the Catholic Church* is a "statement of the church's faith and of Catholic doctrine" (*Fidei Depositum,* 3). In the style of a reference text, the catechism addresses baptism extensively in paragraphs 1210–1284. Paragraphs 1234–1245 offer a "mystagogy of the celebration" of baptism, illustrating how "the meaning and grace of the sacrament of baptism are clearly seen in the rites of its celebration" (#1234).

The *Code of Canon Law* is the body of laws that governs the Roman Catholic Church. Canons 849–878 address baptism. A useful edition is *The Code of Canon Law: A Text and Commentary,* commissioned by the Canon Law Society of America (New York: Paulist Press, 1985). It provides helpful commentary after the text of each canon.

The *Instruction on Infant Baptism,* issued by the Vatican's Sacred Congregation for the Doctrine of the Faith in 1980, summarizes "the principal points of doctrine in this field which justify the church's constant practice down the centuries and demonstrate its permanent value in spite of the difficulties raised today" (#3).

25

Environment and Art in Catholic Worship, a 1978 document from the United States Bishops' Committee on the Liturgy, addresses the baptistry in paragraphs 76–77 and reemphasizes the church's preference for immersion: "To speak of symbols and of sacramental signification is to indicate that immersion is the fuller and more appropriate symbolic action in baptism" (#76). The first four sections of the document offer a worthwhile reflection on symbols, gestures and spatial issues that affect liturgical celebrations.

The *Book of Blessings* is the ritual for the formal blessings by the church. The first chapter of the book contains several blessings related to baptism: the order for the blessing of baptized children, for the blessing of a child not yet baptized, for the blessing of parents before childbirth, for the blessing of a mother before and after childbirth, for the blessing of parents after a miscarriage, and for the blessing of parents and an adopted child. The prayers and symbolic actions of these blessings are important sources of catechetical reflection on baptism.

Catholic Household Blessings and Prayers is designed for use by individual families and households. Sections related to baptism include the blessing for the conception or adoption of a child, the blessing during pregnancy for both parents, and for the mother, the blessing near the time of birth, the thanksgiving for a newborn or newly adopted child, the parents' thanksgiving, the blessing on bringing a child into the home, the mother's blessing of the child when nursing or feeding, the blessing on the anniversary of baptism, and the blessing of parents after a miscarriage. Some of these are contained in Jane Marie Osterholt's article, "A Proposed Method of Liturgy and Catechesis," in chapter 2 of this book.

A Proposed Method of Liturgy and Catechesis

Jane Marie Osterholt

Baptism needs preparation. Through both liturgy and catechesis, the household of the one to be baptized, the parish community and the assembly prepare to celebrate baptism.

The word *liturgy* originally meant "public work" or a "service in the name of or on behalf of the people." In Christian tradition it means the participation of the people of God in "the work of God" (*Catechism of the Catholic Church* [CCC], 1069).

The word *catechesis* means anything that is intended to assist "individuals and communities acquire and deepen Christian faith and identity through initiation rites, instruction, and formation of conscience (National Catechetical Directory [NCD], *Sharing the Light of Faith*, 5).

There is a close relationship between catechesis and liturgy. Both are rooted in the church's faith, and although they do so in different ways, both strengthen faith and both summon Christians to conversion. In the liturgy the church is at prayer, offering adoration, praise and thanksgiving to God and seeking and celebrating reconciliation. Here one finds both an expression of faith and a means for deepening it. Catechesis prepares people for full and active participation in liturgy by helping them understand its nature, rituals and symbols. At the same time, catechesis flows from liturgy; by reflecting on the community's experiences of worship, catechesis seeks to relate those experiences to daily life and to growth in faith (NCD, 1131).

Preparation for baptism includes explaining what the rite of baptism means, why we do what we do, the meaning of the symbols used and the connection between the celebration of the sacrament and the everyday life of a Catholic Christian. To be done well, the rite itself also requires preparation, with time to reflect on the readings and on the meaning of the symbols for each person involved. After the celebration, time needs to be set aside to reflect on what took place and how each person was affected. In this chapter, some options will be proposed not only to assist the preparation by the household, the community and the parish assembly, but also to assist the celebration of the rite, with some questions for reflection.

Preparation for Baptism

Preparation for the Parish

Long-term preparation for baptism might include providing the entire assembly with a series of bulletin articles, supported by preaching or other guidance, on the meaning of the rite of baptism and how it affects each person; workshop sessions, evening presentations, afternoons or evenings of reflection with a similar focus might also be appropriate at various times. For example, an opportunity could be provided each month for members of the parish to gather with the neophytes (newly baptized adults), the parents of children who have been baptized recently, and perhaps the godparents, to reflect on the various aspects and symbols of baptism and to ponder their relationship to everyday experiences.

This would provide a suitable environment for helping parishioners integrate all the elements of the Christian life — community, service, catechesis and liturgy — into a common vision. Finally, all members of the assembly should continually be invited to pray for the households that are preparing for baptism; the names of those to be baptized might be included in the parish bulletin and in the general intercessions of the liturgy.

Preparation of the Household

BLESSINGS AND PRAYERS Ideally, a household's preparation for the baptism of a child begins once the pregnancy or adoption is confirmed. As part of the household's preparation, blessings before the birth can create a welcoming climate. These blessing prayers might be distributed to households anticipating the birth or adoption of a child. By using them, the household could prepare itself spiritually as well as physically and emotionally for the welcome of the new child as well as the baptism. *Catholic Household Blessings and Prayers* ([CHBP] Washington, D.C.: United States Catholic Conference, 1988) includes several appropriate texts, some of which are presented here.

29

The prayer below (CHBP, 216) asks for the conception or adoption of a child and is appropriate for the couple to pray individually, together or with other family members or friends. It may be prayed with Psalm 145:13 – 21.

> God, our creator,
> by your love the world is filled with life,
> through your generosity one generation gives life to another,
> and so are your wonders told and your praises sung.
> We look to you in love and in our need:
> may it be your will that we bear (adopt) a child
>   to share our home and faith.
> Loving God, be close to us
> as we pray to love and do your will.
> You are our God, nourishing us for ever and ever.
> Amen.

During the pregnancy the following blessing for both parents might be prayed when a group of family or friends gathers (CHBP, 219). It may be led by a priest, a deacon or a member of the laity. A scripture reading, such as Luke 1:39–45, may precede it.

> Gracious Father,
> your Word, spoken in love, created the human family
> and your Son, conceived in love, restored it to your friendship.
> Hear the prayers of N. and N.,
> who await the birth of their child.
> Calm their fears when they are anxious.
> Watch over and support these parents
> and bring their child into this world
> safely and in good health,
> so that as members of your family
> they may praise you and glorify you
> through your Son, our Lord Jesus Christ,
> now and forever.
> Amen.

> *(All make the sign of the cross. The leader concludes:)*

> May God, who chose to make known and to send
> the blessings of eternal salvation
> through the motherhood of the Blessed Virgin Mary
> and the protection of Saint Joseph,
> bless us and keep us in his care,
> now and forever.
> Amen.

30

A similar blessing for the mother during pregnancy can be found on page 220 of *Catholic Household Blessings and Prayers*. The following prayer of thanksgiving (CHBP, 224) may be prayed by the parents on first holding a newborn or newly adopted child, on bringing the child home for the first time, or on other occasions before the child's baptism.

Source of all blessings, Protector of infants,
look with favor on this child, N.
Hold him/her gently in your hands.
When he/she is reborn of water and the Holy Spirit,
bring him/her into the church,
there to share in your kingdom
and with us to bless your name for ever.
We ask this through Christ our Lord.
Amen.

(The parents trace the sign of the cross on the child's forehead.)

N., may the Lord Jesus, who loved children,
bless you and keep you in his love,
now and forever.
Amen.

This blessing (CHBP, 226) is appropriate to pray when bringing the child home for the first time.

Good Lord,
you have tenderly loved us,
and given us this home and good friends.
May we make a true home for this child
where he/she will learn trust in us and in you.
(May his/her brothers and sister rejoice
in their own growing up
as they help to care for this child.)
We ask this through Christ our Lord.
Amen.

CHOOSING GODPARENTS As part of the preparation for the baptism of their child, parents need to consider the role and responsibility of godparents. Each of us needs someone to walk with us, to share the story of the scriptures, to show us how faith is lived in everyday life, to be a model of service within the wider community. Walking with the child on the journey of life and faith is the role of the entire

Christian community, but it is a particular responsibility of the child's godparent(s). Parents select one or two persons to assist them in guiding their child on this journey in the practice of faith. Godparents are mentors and guides in faith for the newly baptized. As part of the preparation for their child's baptism, parents might reflect on these questions while selecting a godparent:

> **How will the godparent(s) share in the practice of faith?**
>
> **When will the godparent(s) pray with our child?**
>
> **What role will the godparent(s) have in the everyday life of our child?**
>
> **How will the community be a model of faith in action for our child?**

32

Connecting Rite and Symbol to Everyday Life

Reception of the Children

"This sacrament is called *baptism,* after the central rite by which it is carried out: to baptize (Greek *baptizein*) means to 'plunge' or 'immerse' . . ." (CCC, 1214). As with all the sacraments, baptism is an immersion into the life of Christ, not just for the one being baptized or for the family but for the entire community. Sacraments are for the community. One aspect of the sacrament of baptism is the welcoming of the child in the name of Christ. When one is welcomed in the name of Jesus Christ, all are welcomed. Welcoming takes on many different forms based on the culture and on familial experiences.

NAMING   Most often when we meet someone, we greet that person and introduce ourselves. So too in the rite of baptism. The one to be baptized, the family and godparents are greeted at the door of the church. The celebrant, in the name of the assembled community and the church, asks, "What name do you give (or, have you given) your child?" (*Rite of Baptism for Children* [RBC], 37) so that he or she may be welcomed and received by name into the Christian family. The name that a person is given is the name called by God. As we come to understand this part of the rite, we take time to reflect on its meaning in the life of the community, the parish assembly, the family and the individual.

> **How do we welcome strangers into this parish community?**
>
> **When do we welcome newcomers into our parish?**
>
> **What is the sign of welcome that is given, and who gives it?**
>
> **How do I welcome someone new into my family?**
>
> **What sign of welcome is given to the one to be baptized?**

33

REQUESTING BAPTISM   With the name known, the reception continues: "What do you ask of God's church for (N.?)" (RBC, 37). The parents reply with their intent, which may be stated either as "baptism," "faith," "the grace of Christ," "entrance into the church," "eternal life" or a similar response. The reply is key to understanding the sacrament and the sacramental life of the church. Faith is a mystery we do not fully understand, that we cannot entirely comprehend with our intellect, but that we believe. Entrance into the church is the beginning of the journey of faith, a journey that takes a lifetime and is taken with others. This journey, though it may get lonely and the path may seem unclear, is led by God. Sharing the journey gives occasion for those who have traveled longer to share stories and memories of the gift of faith with the new member.

> **How is the journey shared?**
>
> **Who shares the memories and when are they shared with the new member and the parish community?**

When is the story of my faith shared with other members of the community?

How will we celebrate the beginning of the faith journey of this newest member?

What will we, as a faith community, do to remember this new member, and what will this new member do to remember this welcome?

SIGNING WITH THE CROSS   Faith is demonstrated each day through signs and symbols. The sign of the cross is a prime example. The one to be baptized is signed on the forehead by the celebrant and then by the parent(s) and godparent(s). This signing marks the person as a follower of Jesus Christ. Those belonging to the Catholic Christian community remind themselves of their baptism every time they sign themselves with holy water as they enter or leave the sacred space of worship. This simple gesture is a powerful sign of identification.

34

How do I see the sign of the cross marking me as a follower of Christ?

At what other times might the parents and godparents sign this child with the sign of the cross?

When might the assembled community sign each other?

How might this blessing be incorporated into daily life?

What significance does the sign of the cross have for me?

Celebration of God's Word

PROCLAMATION OF THE SCRIPTURES   The sign of the cross is a tremendous reminder for all Christians of the great love Jesus has for us. That love is shared through the celebration of God's word as we are invited to hear and reflect on the power of the scripture readings in our daily lives. The stories we read and hear speak of God's interaction with people like ourselves, but in a different time and place. The newly baptized are invited to make the scriptures an integral part of their lives, as are we. We might ask ourselves:

> **What meaning does this passage have in my life?**
>
> **How does this reading affect the child to be baptized?**
>
> **How might this community of faith be challenged by this reading?**
>
> **Where will this scripture be lived out in my life and in the life of this community?**

LITANY OF THE SAINTS   We pray for the one to be baptized as well as for the community, remembering those holy men and women who have gone before us, who have lived out the word of God in their lives. Through the litany of the saints, we are reminded of those persons, and we are invited to recall the witness they bore through their lives to the power of God alive within and around them. The litany of saints is a sign of the connection that we have through the ages with these holy mentors.

> **Who are the people we remember in the litany of saints? Who are the holy ones who have gone before me that have touched my life?**
>
> **How did they live the gospel?**
>
> **How might this litany be a reminder to me and to this community of our connectedness?**
>
> **How might this litany be incorporated into my daily life?**

EXORCISM AND ANOINTING   In remembering those who have journeyed this path of faith, we know that their lives were tested by the power of evil. In the prayer of exorcism, the church asks that the one to be baptized be freed of the evil one and filled with new life. The anointing with the oil of catechumens is used to mark this person as one called by God and filled with the power of God: "We anoint you with the oil of salvation in the name of Christ our Savior; may he strengthen you with his power, who lives and reigns for ever and ever. Amen" (RBC, 50).

> **Oil has been used through the centuries as a sign of God's favor. How is oil a sign for me of God's power?**
>
> **What purpose does blessed oil have in my life?**
>
> **Have I been blessed with oil?**
>
> **After this celebration, how will oil speak to me of baptism and initiation into God?**

LAYING ON OF HANDS   Oil is one of the many signs and symbols used not only in baptism but also in the celebration of confirmation, the anointing of the sick and the ordination of priests and bishops. In addition, the laying on of hands is a powerful sign of God's healing and presence. In the rite of baptism, the celebrant, in silence, lays his hands on the person to be baptized, reminding us of Jesus reaching out and touching in gentleness and love the children and those gathered around him.

> **How might we be models of Jesus' gentleness and love?**
>
> **When did I last experience the healing touch of God through the hands of another?**
>
> **How might the hands of this one to be baptized touch me? Have I reflected on my own hands and the power that is in them?**
>
> **How might we, as a parish community, touch the lives of others in love?**

Celebration of the Sacrament

BLESSING OF THE BAPTISMAL WATER   Through the celebration of the sacrament of baptism, the lives of many are touched by the power of God—not only the one to be baptized but also the parents, siblings, godparents, relatives and friends and the entire parish community. The blessing and invocation of God over the baptismal water evokes in us the feeling of being washed, of being cleansed, of being given life, of having our thirst quenched. Water, so often taken for granted, is blessed and made holy.

What do I do with water every day?

How do I respect the gift of water?

How does water nourish and sustain me?

When do I use holy water?

When do we as a parish community bless and use water?

RENUNCIATION OF SIN AND PROFESSION OF FAITH   Sometimes the presence of water can frighten us and concern us, and we become overwhelmed and forget the saving power of God. Those of us who have already been baptized are invited to renounce sin and to renew our own profession of faith. We profess what we believe as a reminder to ourselves that we, too, have been called to follow Christ and to give witness in our daily lives to the power of God as we say no to the power of the evil one.

What do I believe?

How do I live each day as a result of this belief?

When do I support and challenge myself and others to practice this belief?

How will I model this faith to the newly baptized?

Where will this parish community witness what it professes?

BAPTISM   The assembled community is reminded through the profession of faith of what we believe and of what we invite this new member to accept and believe. After the community's assent, the child is formally welcomed in baptism as the water is poured over his or her head three times or as the person is immersed in the water three times to signify the Trinity, the mystery of God. "I baptize you in the name of the Father, and of the Son, and of the Holy Spirit" (RBC, 60).

> **When do I sign myself with the words of baptism?**
>
> **As I sign myself, do I remember the profession of faith that I made?**
>
> **Do I celebrate the anniversary of my welcome into God's family by baptism?**
>
> **How will we, as a family, celebrate each person's baptismal anniversary?**
>
> **How can we, as a parish, remember baptismal anniversaries?**

38

ANOINTING WITH CHRISM   As the water is a sign of the healing and cleansing power of God, the chrism with which the newly baptized is anointed on the crown of the head is a sign of having a share in God's glory. Through this anointing, the newly baptized is acclaimed to be priestly, prophetic and royal like Christ, the one anointed priest, prophet and king. What a strong sign — to be marked as one of God's chosen ones, with the role and responsibility of a priest who invites others to pray; a prophet who challenges others to live in solidarity with the poor and oppressed; and a ruler who leads by power of baptism.

> **How am I priestly, prophetic and royal?**
>
> **When do I invite myself and others to pray?**
>
> **When do I challenge myself and others to live in solidarity with the poor and oppressed?**
>
> **When do I lead others through example and humility?**

How will I witness this commitment to the newly baptized?

CLOTHING WITH THE WHITE GARMENT   In addition to being marked with the oil of chrism as one chosen, the newly baptized is clothed with a white garment. "The white garment symbolizes that the person baptized has 'put on Christ,' has risen with Christ" (CCC, 1243). The white garment is symbolic of new life in Christ, both at the beginning and end of a person's life. What we wear gives a sign to others of how we perceive ourselves. Our clothing gives the outward appearance of what we feel on the inside.

What does the white garment say to you?

How do clothes say who you are?

What do you want your clothes to say about you?

How can your clothes remind you of your baptism?

What kind of clothes do you wear to the Sunday liturgy?

39

PRESENTATION OF THE LIGHTED CANDLE   In addition to being given the white garment, the newly baptized is given a candle that has been lighted from the Easter candle.

> Parents and godparents, this light is entrusted to you to be kept burning brightly. These children of yours have been enlightened by Christ. They are to walk always as children of the light. May they keep the flame of faith alive in their hearts. When the Lord comes, may they go out to meet him with all the saints in the heavenly kingdom. (RBC, 64)

This candle is symbolic of the light of Christ, which the newly baptized is now asked to shine forth in daily life, just as each of us is asked to do. As we reflect on our own baptism and the light of Christ that was given to us, we ask ourselves:

What does the light of Christ mean to me?

What role does light have in my life?

When do I light my baptismal candle?

When do we as a church use candles and for what purpose?

How can we become the light of Christ to our local community?

EPHPHETHA   In the giving of the garment and the candle, the newly baptized is designated as one with the responsibility to proclaim the Good News of Jesus Christ. Having received both these symbols, the newly baptized then receives a special blessing, the "Ephphetha," or prayer over the ears and mouth, through which the senses are blessed so that the newly baptized might hear the word of God and speak it: "The Lord Jesus made the deaf hear and the dumb speak. May he soon touch your ears to receive his word, and your mouth to proclaim his faith, to the praise and glory of God the Father. Amen" (RBC, 65).

40

How do I hear the word of God?

How do we as a parish assembly hear the word of God?

How will we proclaim the word of God to this newly baptized child?

When and where will I speak the word of God?

When and where will we, as an assembly, speak the word of God?

LOOKING FORWARD TO CONFIRMATION AND EUCHARIST   Having received this blessing and the command not only to hear God's word but also to proclaim it, the rite of baptism is concluded. If the baptism does not take place within the eucharist, those assembled gather near the altar to demonstrate the intimate connection of baptism with confirmation and eucharist as sacraments of initiation.

These children have been reborn in baptism. They are now called children of God, for so indeed they are. In confirmation they will receive the fullness of God's Spirit. In holy communion they will share the banquet of Christ's sacrifice, calling God their Father in the midst of the church. In their name . . . let us pray together in the words our Lord has given us: Our Father. . . . (RBC, 68–69)

BLESSING OF THE PARENTS   Having prayed the Lord's Prayer, we conclude the rite with a special blessing first for the mothers, then for the fathers and, lastly, for the entire assembly. These last parts of the rite invite us to reflect on the importance of prayer and of praying together with the newly baptized, the parents, the godparents and the entire assembly. Prayer is our conversation with God and the bond that unites us as one. The power of prayer and the energy received are God's gift to us.

Do we take time to pray for the newly baptized and the family?

How do we understand prayer and sacraments in the life of this parish, the church?

What place do the sacraments and prayer have in my life?

When do we gather to pray as a family, as a parish community?

How will we pray with the newly baptized?

41

Prayer is integral not only to the rite but also to the preparation process. Many parishes have an extensive preparation period to facilitate the meaningful celebration of the rite by all the participants: the one to be baptized, the parents, godparents, family members, relatives, friends and the assembly.

Reflection

The actual celebration of baptism, to be meaningful, needs not only preparation and prayer but also active participation and involvement, which includes singing, sharing in the responses and blessings, silence and reverential participation. Following the celebration of the rite, a period of reflection on what transpired is encouraged. This may take place immediately before the assembled community leaves or within a week after the celebration. During this reflection time, all are invited to share what they experienced during the rite. Some possible questions that would lead to personal and communal sharing might be:

What did you experience; what touched your heart?

What did this baptism mean to your daily life?

How did you affirm your own baptism through this celebration?

How was the assembled community involved?

How will you, as an individual and as a parish, act differently because of this celebration of baptism?

How will your life as an individual and as a parish be transformed as a result of being called and sent by the power of God through baptism?

We ask ourselves the fundamental questions: How did I experience the work of God (liturgy), and how did I deepen my Christian faith and identity (catechesis)? In taking the time to ponder what has happened, we have named the working of God in our lives and have been shaped by the experience so that we act in such a way that our lives reflect that we indeed walk by the light of faith.

Infant Baptism, Catechesis and the Catechetical Process

Patricia Hawkins Vaillancourt

The birth of a baby is one of life's most profound moments. Many new parents consider it a moment when they feel the presence of God in such a special way that even many years later they go back to it as a time of knowing or understanding the awesomeness, the power, the beauty and especially the love of God. It is a sacramental moment, a revelatory moment in family life. Sadly, it is also a moment that people often do not connect with church.

Catechesis for infant baptism can enable parents to make the important connections. It can also help them see the tremendous need we all have for the church, the people of God. Infant baptism celebrates this new God-given life by welcoming the child into the community of believers. Catechesis enhances the family's participation in this celebration.

What Is Catechesis?

The National Catechetical Directory (NCD) tells us that

> Catechesis refers to efforts which help individuals and
> communities acquire and deepen Christian faith and
> identity through initiation rites, instruction and formation
> of conscience. It includes both the message presented
> and the way in which it is presented. (#5)

Four important concepts flow from this broad definition: informal
catechesis, formal catechesis, catechetical content and catechetical
process. These concepts must be understood in order to catechize
parents effectively.

Informal Catechesis

Informal catechesis is not planned. It flows from the lives of
people of faith, in their reflection, in their conversation, in their reading and in their sharing of their lives. Committed married couples
catechize each other when they discuss such things as the role
God plays in their lives, the meaning of a Sunday homily, what a
particular scripture passage means or how they will celebrate
Christmas more prayerfully. Parents catechize their children when,
in faith, they answer the simple questions all children ask about
life and death, or when they read stories to their children about
people of faith or high moral conviction. They also catechize when
they use home rituals such as the Advent wreath, or when they
display a crucifix or other religious art in their home. They catechize
most powerfully when their actions witness to their children the
words of the scriptures. Informal catechesis takes place when
mothers discuss, over a cup of coffee, how they teach their children
to be kind to each other, how to create a more loving home, how
to find time to read and reflect and pray more frequently, or how
to help a child break a bad habit or come to know God more deeply.

Informal catechesis, this sharing of faith and life, is the glue
that holds Christian families together and cements them to
the parish church. It is contained in the daily interaction within
families of faith and between families of faith in homes, in parks,

in the workplace and, of course, on the church grounds. The National Catechetical Directory explains it this way:

> Parents are the first and foremost catechists of their children. They catechize informally but powerfully by example and instruction. They communicate values and attitudes by showing love for Christ and his church and for each other, by reverently receiving the eucharist and living in its spirit, and by fostering justice and love in all their relationships. Their active involvement in the parish, their readiness to seek opportunities to serve others, and their practice of frequent and spontaneous prayer, all make meaningful their professions of belief. Parents nurture faith in their children by showing them the richness and beauty of lived faith. (#212)

This informal catechesis is the call, the responsibility, the lifestyle that these parents have chosen for their family when they entered Christian marriage and again when choosing baptism for their child. The church community has, in return, a responsibility to assist them in this endeavor. Infant baptism preparation can provide the motivation for parents to begin this kind of informal catechesis.

45

Formal Catechesis

Formal catechesis is planned catechesis. It takes place when a group of adults comes together for Bible study, marriage enrichment, Christian parenting or other such classes. It is part of all family sacramental preparations, Catholic school religion classes and children's after-school religion programs. Planned catechesis focuses on specific content and includes a plan for presenting the material. Formal catechesis also assists people in assimilating that content. It can take place in one or more sessions or courses or, as in the case of children, over a period of many years.

In preparing parents and godparents for infant baptism, formal catechesis usually entails several planned sessions in which parents or expectant parents are brought together to explore content appropriate to the sacrament of baptism and to the establishment or enchancement of Christian family life.

Catechetical Content

Catechetical content is the subject matter to be taught. It is generally drawn from the scriptures, church doctrine and Catholic tradition. When parents and godparents are being prepared for an infant's baptism, the content can include such topics as the meaning of baptism and the sacraments in general, an understanding of church, an explanation of original sin and an exploration of the *Rite of Baptism for Children*. Content also can include practical assistance in developing faith, both within individuals and within the family as a unit.

Catechetical Process

Catechetical process is "the way in which the message is presented" (NCD, 5). It is a way to help people internalize what is taught. People retain only about five to ten percent of what they hear and carry into their lives only a portion of what they retain. Catechetical process allows people to look at information in a variety of ways through sharing, discussion, reflection and planned action. It is a process because it goes on continually. We listen, we hear, we discard, we compare, we choose, and we act. Catechetical process facilitates this life process by giving us time to explore information in a variety of ways, to make it truly our own.

Good baptismal catechesis includes all four of these essentials. It provides time for, and assistance with, informal catechesis and also plans formal catechetical sessions that include significant catechetical content and carefully designed catechetical process.

Family Perspective

From a family perspective, there are two other important concepts that should underlie any ministry with parents and/or children: The family is a "domestic church," and faith and conversion are lifelong journeys.

Domestic Church

The National Catechetical Directory refers to the family as a "domestic church," that is, the "church in miniature" (#226). The domestic church, the church of the home, is the primary community in which parents raise their children. It is the only community that has the capacity to tend consistently to the basic needs of love and nurturance from birth until death. In today's mobile society, families frequently move in and out of other communities to which they belong. The family has the capacity to provide stability and ongoing faith development throughout a person's life. As people move from parish to parish or from one part of the country to another, the family is not only the source of continuity and growth but also the vehicle that will (or will not) link itself to the parish community. This is true even when the family itself is divided by death or divorce. Newly single parents provide continuity while working out some kind of accommodation to their changed status. The family, the domestic church, even while under such great strain, still continues to be responsible for providing the basic economic, psychological, emotional and faith needs of its members.

47

This church of the home, this domestic church, needs parish support. Baptismal catechesis is an important place to begin the ongoing connection and catechesis that can truly support Catholic family life.

Lifelong Journeys

From the perspective of the family, another important concept underlying catechesis is the understanding that both faith and conversion are ongoing, lifelong journeys. While growth and development are certainly apparent in children, the concept is no less important in regard to adults.

Many parents come to the church at this time in their early adulthood with little understanding of either their faith or the reasons why baptism is important for their child and their family. So it is an opportune time to assist them in their journey of faith. The birth of a baby, especially if it is a couple's first child, requires a shift in every member's role in the family. Reflection on family change and the role of faith in that process can assist with ongoing conversion.

For adults who have committed themselves to the vocation of marriage, the most compelling and powerful conversion almost always takes place within the long-term relationships of family life. Who better than a spouse knows those areas in an individual's life that need more virtue, more holiness — in other words, conversion. Spouses are called by virtue of their marriage vows and their baptismal promises to lead each other to holiness. Love, kindness, patience, fidelity, truthfulness — all the virtues — begin at home between spouses and develop within relationships with children.

This kind of growth is a lifelong journey, and every family is at a different point on that path. This must be taken into account when planning prebaptismal and postbaptismal catechesis. These programs should be designed to meet the growth needs of every family taking part, regardless of where they are on their faith journey. Thus a variety of approaches must be offered at each juncture of the program: during a home visit, at coffee time and certainly during group meetings.

Catechesis can and should be an integral part of every phase of a program designed for parents who want to have their child baptized. Informal catechesis takes place every time there is contact with the parents or prospective parents. Sometimes the most profound catechetical moments take place in one-on-one conversation between a baptismal team member and a parent on the telephone or over coffee at a formal meeting. These moments are extremely important because they address issues of immediacy for the family involved; therefore, they should be dealt with in a respectful manner and as soon as possible.

Carefully chosen catechetical materials, over and above the program materials, should also be available at every step along the way. Adults do read, and reading is a primary means of obtaining both information and material for reflection. One only has to look at the number of flourishing new bookstores, their shelves overflowing with self-help books to understand how adults go about informing and converting themselves. Baptismal teams and parishes in general would be wise to take advantage of this growing phenomenon by providing written materials, such as inexpensive booklets, on topics of interest to young families as their faith needs arise. Free booklets and materials can be provided to parents when the baptismal team visits, at the formal catechetical sessions and even in the parish book rack. Books and other materials for purchase (without pressure to buy) can also be made available at various times during the program.

It is best to plan formal catechesis around the "family agenda." Parents do most of their preparation for a new baby before the baby is born, when the family is less pressured. Once the infant is on the scene, a whole array of complications arise that make it much more difficult for parents to give adequate time to preparation. Nursing infants require quite a bit of time before they settle into a routine, and sleepless nights become the norm. New babies cannot be left with a young sitter, and if grandparents, older relatives, or full-time infant care are not nearby and readily available, most parents hesitate to leave their infants. There is also the stress involved in shifting family responsibilities so that the family can provide around-the-clock care every day for an infant. The family's agenda once the infant is born is understandably filled with confusion and simple hard work. New parents are tired, very tired. Offering expectant parents the option of beginning their infant baptism preparation during pregnancy gives both parents and the parish a more reasonable period of time for the prayer, reflection and presentation of information needed for spiritual growth to take place.

49

Catechetical Group Sessions

In planning any catechetical group session, three very practical things should be taken into consideration. The first of these is meeting length, the second is the size of the group, and the third is the place where the meeting or meetings will be held.

Time

One and one-half hours is a good time frame to consider when planning, especially when meetings will be held in the evening. The time can be broken up into smaller segments for welcoming and introductions, prayer, information, reflection and/or discussion and informal fellowship over coffee.

Begin and end promptly at the stated times. If at the end of the session people wish to stay for a second cup of coffee, they should be encouraged to do so. This can be a special time for informal catechesis, but ending the formal part of the sessions on time is especially important for participants who have babysitters.

Size of Group

Groups also should be kept small. Eight or ten parents plus a minimum of two but possibly three or four baptismal team members should be present (e.g., two couples, a couple and a single parent, or a parent and a staff member). At least one team member should be trained in and comfortable with facilitating a group. The others can be there to provide support, to learn facilitation skills through observation or simply to host the meeting.

Welcoming Atmosphere

Meetings should be held in a comfortable, warm and inviting atmosphere. A school cafeteria, gymnasium or classroom suitable for children does not lend itself to adult catechesis. Adults learn best in a home-like atmosphere with an official host/hostess, comfortable seating and warm hospitality. Team members' homes are often the ideal place for meetings, since all of these things are already present. If a family is hosting a meeting in its home, it may be best if other team members lead the meeting itself. When meetings are held on the parish grounds, there should be at least one room specially furnished and equipped where small groups of adults can meet with comfort and ease. It is important that parents be welcomed and addressed as adults and not be made to feel that they are stepping back into their childhood.

Have coffee, tea and finger food available as people arrive. This, along with books to peruse and free leaflets or booklets to take home, creates a welcoming atmosphere and an excellent setting for conversation and fellowship to begin as the host and/or hostess wait for stragglers to arrive. Participants can bring their coffee with them to the group when the session begins.

Introductions are an important part of this atmosphere. Not only should participants be introduced to each other as they arrive, but before the session begins, time should be allowed for each person (team members included) to introduce themselves and tell a little of their story — who they are and any information they care to share. The host or facilitator can begin this informal sharing, thereby serving as a model. Name tags should be made available, and their use encouraged.

51

Content

What will be presented at catechetical sessions should be carefully thought out. It can include some information about baptism, Christian family life and the *Rite of Baptism for Children* itself, with the latter presented after the baby's birth and in close proximity to the actual baptism. All information should be accurate and attractively presented. Resources can include videos, informal speakers or written material. In choosing materials, however, the first requirement is that they adequately present the content which has been chosen for the session.

Catechetical Process

Information, however, is only one part of the catechesis. Good catechesis also requires that the participant is assisted in bringing the information into his or her heart and in finding ways to act upon it. Catechetical process is used to do just that. It seeks to reach into the hearts of people to help them grow, not only in their knowledge and understanding of God but also in their love for God. People need time to digest new information before it becomes their own and thus can prompt them to change their lives. Catechetical process is a format designed to cause reflection, discussion and the opening up of new ways for the future.

Good catechetical process presumes that the catechetical content is carefully prepared and presented either prior to using the process or within the process itself. This can be done in a variety of ways. Lecture and/or video seem to be the simplest and most preferred methods, but creativity should not be discouraged. Role playing, storytelling, combinations of the use of overhead projectors and lecture, and slides taken in the parish of its activities and people are other options.

Prayer and/or ritual need to be part of every gathering. We are a church community, and God is present "where two or more are gathered in God's name." Not only should it be recognized, but even more to the point, it should be established that sacramental preparation is a prayerful journey and a time of grace for each family (the domestic church) and for the parish community. This call to prayer also needs careful preparation by the parish team. The prepared prayer should flow from the baptism ritual itself, using the symbols and promises in an adult format.

Good catechetical process also requires the formulation of thought-provoking questions that flow from the information presented, with the goal of assimilating the information into the participant's life. There is a subtle difference between a discussion question and a reflection question: Both refer back to the information presented, but discussion questions help clarify or increase the available information. Reflection questions, in contrast, probe the individual's (or the couple's) life. Because such questions can at times be threatening, careful wording is necessary. Participants should never be required to share. The person who just wishes to listen should be free to do so. Also, writing responses (journaling) can be much less threatening than verbal participation, particularly when responses are shared at home between spouses or between parents and godparents.

Reflection questions can never be answered with a simple yes or no. They are meant to probe the beliefs or experiences that motivate people's actions. Their purpose is to give participants a clear understanding of themselves and their beliefs. These questions are open-ended and produce a variety of responses for the group to think about. Some good lead-in words and phrases for open-ended, thought-provoking questions are "Describe _____," "Think about a time when _____," "What do you think about _____?" or "How did you feel when _____?"

After the questions have been formulated, they should be typed or written on a separate piece of paper for each participant. There should be space for written responses after each question. The content of the questions flows from the catechetical material being presented and therefore brings the content into the beliefs and experiences of the group.

There should be an interplay between the formulation of the questions and how they are to be used. Reflection questions can be used in a number of ways, and this should be kept in mind as they are formulated. Some questions can and should be sent home with the participants to be used in planning their new ways of being committed Christian parents.

A Sample Process

Here is an example of an effective catechetical process that would take about 45 minutes.

1. *Reflective presentation and written response.* Begin with a short anecdote, a story from personal experience, literature or other material, or even a slide reflection that will draw attention to the material to be presented. This is followed by a private, written reflection on questions that focus on the session's catechetical content. These questions probe the participants' memories and experiences. (Written reflection is an important part of the process because it allows each participant time to collect his or her thoughts. It also gives even the quietest people an opportunity to express themselves, even if they choose not to share what they have written.) After writing their responses, the participants keep them for later use.

2. *Presentation of the catechetical content.*

3. *Private, written reflection* on questions that ask participants to respond to the material.

4. *Comparison of responses.* Participants are then asked to compare and contrast their two sets of responses and comment on this. This can also be a written response to reflective questions.

5. *Small-group sharing.* When writing and reflection are completed, the participants are asked to form groups of three, four or five people to share their thoughts on the questions or on what they have written. No one should be forced to share if they prefer not to do so. People usually find it fairly easy to respond in simple conversation with such a small number of people.

6. *Interaction with the facilitator and the larger group.* This is more of a reporting situation, and its nature is set by the facilitator stating simply, "We always like to hear what different groups have been saying about this topic. Would someone like to share what was talked about in your group?" Then give people time to think. Usually the more vocal people respond without taking ownership of the view. They say things such as, "One of the things we talked about was _____." This opens discussion to the larger group and still gives people a measure of anonymity in regard to their

personal reflections. It also creates a non-threatening atmosphere for sharing.

7. *Quick summary by the facilitator* of what was said, with review of important catechetical content (about one minute).

8. *Take-home reflection questions* either for the couple to work on together or for parents and godparents to share at their leisure. These questions are directed toward the future home environment and the faith development of the parents and any older children the parent(s) may have.

This catechetical process can be adapted for private reflection at home by eliminating the interaction of the facilitator with the large group, by having the small-group interaction take place at home between spouses (in the case of a single parent, a godparent or other adult can reflect and share), by adding catechetical content and by giving very specific written instructions on each step of the process. Interaction with the larger church community is, however, a vital part of catechesis and cannot be eliminated completely.

The Importance of Catechists

Perhaps the single most important element for good catechesis during the baptismal process is a team of well-informed and faith-filled catechists. Catechists serve as models and give witness to the Catholic Christian life for these young families. They catechize by who they are as well as by what they say and do. It is important that they be prayerful people who are able to express their love of God and their faith in simple language.

In preparing catechists for baptismal ministry, one of the most important things to be addressed is the catechist's own prayer life and faith journey. This can be done by providing ongoing enrichment and faith development for all team members.

Catechists need to be familiar with the questions commonly raised by parents and should feel comfortable enough in their knowledge to be able to address these issues. Complex questions can always be brought to a member of the parish staff. Catechists must be able to listen with compassion and deal sensitively with whatever views are expressed by the program's participants, and they need to be welcoming, hospitable people who can support and affirm others without compromising Catholic teaching. Catechists can be taught facilitation skills and how to utilize catechetical process. They can be given an understanding of adult-learning requirements and of the need for catechetical processes which flow from those requirements.

After catechists have been given the formation and information needed for their task, the next step is practical experience. The most effective and easiest way to train catechists is to engage them in an on-site training internship. By working with someone who is a skilled catechist and by listening and observing how the various processes work, catechists can learn firsthand the skills needed. After each working session or visit, there should be some reflection on all that has taken place. Catechists should also be part of the planning process so that they are fully aware of each step in the process and can pass this information on to parents as needed.

Catechists who work in the infant-baptism ministry of parishes usually find this to be one of the most rewarding of all the ministries available to them. They find that new babies are very special people, and that their parents are a joy to work with.

When to Celebrate Baptism

Linda Gaupin

P rior to the liturgical reforms inaugurated by the Second Vatican Council, the question of when to celebrate baptism was relatively simple. The infant normally was brought to the church soon after birth and baptized at a quasi-private celebration in the back of church on a Sunday afternoon, when few people were present.

Since the promulgation of the *Rite of Baptism for Children* (RBC), however, several issues have arisen concerning when to celebrate baptism. These issues run the gamut from the appropriate liturgical season and the most suitable day of the week, to the celebration of baptism within Mass or outside Mass. None of these are superficial concerns; they go to the heart of the liturgical renewal generated by the Second Vatican Council in the *Constitution on the Sacred Liturgy*. This is especially true for baptism, because the question of when to celebrate baptism is intimately connected with issues that pertain to the revision of the liturgical year.

Time of Year

One of the more debatable points concerns identifying the appropriate times of the year for the celebration of baptism for children who have not reached catechetical age. Some argue that baptism should be reserved only to the Easter Vigil, or at least the Easter season. Others allow that it should be celebrated in the parish three, four or five times a year, and that these times should be in accord with the nature of the season or feast (for example, Christmas season, Easter season, Trinity Sunday). Still others have raised serious concerns about the practice of celebrating baptism (as well as confirmation and first communion) during Lent, since this practice goes against the spirit and purpose of the lenten season as a time of preparation for baptism and a time for repentance.

Arguments against reserving the celebration of baptism to certain times of the year are more often rooted in practical concerns than theological ones, although theological concerns also play a role in this discussion. In some regions where the number of baptisms on a given Sunday is relatively large, opponents to restricting the celebration of baptism to the Easter season or even to certain times of the year argue that it would be impossible to accommodate the large numbers of faithful who bring their children for baptism. Others point out that no law exists forbidding the celebration of baptism during Lent or restricting its celebration to certain times.

The directives given in the *Rite of Baptism for Children* on the time and place for the baptism of children often bring more confusion than clarity to this topic. On the one hand, the rite states that "to bring out the paschal character of baptism, it is recommended that the sacrament be celebrated *during the Easter Vigil* or on a Sunday, when the church commemorates the Lord's resurrection" (#9). But the rite also states that "an infant should be baptized within the first weeks after birth" (#8.3). (This latter directive is the basis of the argument put forth by those who favor the celebration of baptism at any time during the liturgical year.)

Although these conflicting statements appear to cancel each other out, there is reasonable cause to promote the celebration of baptism of children who have not reached catechetical age at the Easter Vigil or during the Easter season. From earliest times, the church gave precedence to the celebration of baptism at Easter, even when the candidates for baptism were mostly infants or young children. When different regions of Europe began to abandon this practice, local councils tried to curb the change in this time-honored tradition. For example, the Council of Auxerre issued the following canon in the year 578:

> It is forbidden to baptize at any time except the Easter service, except in the case of those who are near to death and those whom they call bedridden. And if anyone living in another district shall after this interdict contumaciously bring his children to be baptized in our churches, let them not be received, and any presbyter who shall presume to receive them shall be banned from the communion of the church for three months.[1]

Furthermore, even when baptisms were celebrated at times other than Easter, the church continued to restrict the celebration during the season of Lent. Baptistries were shut and sealed with the bishop's ring during Lent so that the paschal character of baptism would be preserved. This is wonderfully illustrated in a canon issued by the seventeenth Council of Toledo in the year 732:

> At the beginning of Lent the mystery of baptism is universally restricted, and it is necessary as the church's custom requires that the doors of the baptistry should then be shut by the bishop's hand and sealed with his ring, and under no circumstances opened until Maundy Thursday is celebrated: The reason is that it should be universally declared by the bishop's seal that during this season baptism and sanctification cannot be administered, except in the most serious cases of necessity; and again, when the bishop opens the door it may signify the mystery of the Lord's resurrection in which an entry upon life was made for humanity, that as he is dead and buried with Christ in baptism, so he may rise with him again in the glory of God. And because in some churches the bishops take very little trouble to perform and preserve this holy custom, therefore through this our statement we determine and decree that it shall be preserved by the bishops through-out all Spain and Gaul, so that on the aforesaid day, that is, at the beginning of Lent, the doors of the holy baptistry

shall be shut at the end of Lauds and sealed by the bishops
with their rings; and they shall not be opened until
Maundy Thursday is celebrated, when according to custom
the altar cloths are removed. For it is not fitting that
the baptistry should be open to all at a time when it is
forbidden to baptize.[2]

When the rites for baptism were revised following the council,
the time-honored practice of celebrating the sacrament at the
Easter Vigil was restored. The *Rite of Christian Initiation of Adults*
(RCIA) clearly sets forth Easter as the primary time for the
celebration of the initiation sacraments. "The celebration of the
sacraments of Christian initiation should take place at the Easter
Vigil itself."[3] This holds true for older catechumens as well as
for children of catechetical age. The section devoted to the initiation
of children who have reached catechetical age states that "in order
to bring out the paschal character of baptism, celebration of the
sacraments of initiation should preferably take place at the Easter
Vigil or on a Sunday, the day that the church devotes to the
remembrance of Christ's resurrection."[4]

The *Rite of Christian Initiation of Adults* is normative for the
celebration of all the initiation sacraments in the church. Therefore
it is not surprising that the *Rite of Baptism for Children* also
emphasizes the importance of Easter for the celebration of
this sacrament with children who have not reached catechetical age.

Neither rite forbids the celebration of baptism outside Easter,
but Easter is considered the proper time for baptism. It is
interesting to note that the *Rite of Christian Initiation of Adults*
discusses this issue under the topic of "Proper or Usual Times" and
then proceeds to provide norms for the celebration of baptism at
times other than the Easter Vigil under the heading of "Outside the
Usual Times." In this latter instance, when Christian initiation
cannot take place at the Easter Vigil, preference is first given to
choosing a day during the Easter season and then "as far as
possible, the sacraments of initiation are to be celebrated on a
Sunday."[5] The *Rite of Baptism for Children* provides a similar order

60

of preference. "To bring out the paschal character of baptism, it is recommended that the sacrament be celebrated during the Easter Vigil or on Sunday, when the church commemorates the Lord's resurrection" (RBC, 9). In light of this, it is not unreasonable that parishes (or dioceses) would at least strive to have norms that promote the celebration of the baptism of children who have not reached catechetical age during "proper or usual times" of the year.

Day of the Week

Whether baptism is celebrated during the Easter season or at other appropriate times during the year, there is no doubt that Sunday is the preferred day of the week for its celebration.[6] Sunday, the "Lord's Day," the "first day of the week," is the premier day when Christians gather to celebrate the resurrection of the Lord. Sunday underscores the paschal character of baptism and is the appropriate day for it because Sunday enables the faithful to realize more fully that baptism is a sharing in the Lord's passover from death to life. Although the celebration of baptism is not prohibited on weekdays (RBC, 30), the rite clearly states that Sunday should be preferred because it is "the day on which the church celebrates the paschal mystery" (RBC, 32).

61

Within Mass or Outside Mass

The rite also suggests that when baptism is celebrated on Sunday, "it may be celebrated even during Mass, so that the entire community may be present and the relationship between baptism and the eucharist may be clearly seen; but this should not be done too often" (RBC, 9). The question of celebrating baptism during Mass on Sunday has also been the subject of much discussion. The English translation of the rite for use in the United States does not provide a separate chapter for the option of celebrating baptism within Mass, but the Introduction to the *Rite of Baptism for*

Children does provide guidelines for the inclusion of baptism during the Mass (RBC, 29).

On the one hand, the celebration of baptism within Mass when a congregation is present highlights the communal and ecclesial nature of baptism, sets forth its intimate relationship with the eucharist, and underscores the importance and obligations of the "people of God, that is, the church made present by the local community" (RBC, 4). Parishes where baptism is regularly celebrated within Mass, especially on Sunday, attest to the sign value of this practice for the entire parish community.

On the other hand, when baptism is celebrated within Mass, many of the components of the rite, such as the four processions with accompanying song, are not given due attention for fear of prolonging the eucharistic celebration. From another perspective, however, the celebration of baptism during Mass is not the primary issue; that such practice obscures fundamental issues of sacramental practice related to the integral nature of baptism is the issue. Some argue that because first communion is delayed in the Latin rite for a child baptized in infancy, celebrating baptism within Mass only emphasizes the discontinuity between baptism and eucharist.

The primary issue then is the very nature of baptism as "the sacrament of the church's faith and of incorporation into the people of God" (RBC, 10). In order to bring out more fully the ecclesial nature of baptism, the presence of the faithful is of paramount importance. For this reason the rite presumes the presence of the local community, which "has an important role to play in the baptism of both children and adults" (RBC, 4). Unfortunately, in too many places the local community is present only at the Sunday celebration of the eucharist. In these instances, baptism within Mass at least enables the celebration of the rite with the local community present. In fact, the community plays an important role not only in the celebration of the sacrament, but before and afterwards as well.

The *Constitution on the Sacred Liturgy* clearly states that "liturgical services are not private functions, but are celebrations belonging to the church" (#26). It is apparent, however, that there are times when we celebrate the revised rites with a preconciliar, privatized notion of church and sacrament. The *Rite of Baptism for Children* intentionally lists the "Rite of Baptism for Several Children" (chapter 1) before the "Rite of Baptism for One Child" (chapter 2); it also provides a "Rite of Baptism for a Large Number of Children" (chapter 3). And the *Constitution on the Sacred Liturgy* notes that "whenever rites, according to their specific nature, make provision for communal celebration involving the presence and active participation of the faithful, it is to be stressed that this way of celebrating them is to be preferred, as far as possible, to a celebration that is individual and, so to speak, private" (#27).

Privatization of the liturgy also permeates our celebrations of baptism for children when these celebrations of baptism outside Mass take place without music, with few, if any, liturgical ministers and with the expectation that the service will be completed within a relatively brief period of time. In many cases they resemble the preconciliar celebration of baptism, with the exceptions that a few more people are present and that the baptism is not performed in the back of the church. In some cases, pastoral practice allows more than one celebration of baptism on a given Sunday, each of which is accommodated to an individual family, even though the General Introduction to the *Rite of Christian Initiation of Adults* states that "as far as possible, all recently born babies should be baptized at a common celebration on the same day. Except for a good reason, baptism should not be celebrated more than once on the same day in the same church" (#27).

Reserving baptism to the Easter season or even to specific times of the year may result in large numbers of children being baptized in a single celebration and an even larger number of faithful present. But it also brings the faithful—the family, relatives, friends and even members of the local community—together as church to

63

take an active part in the communal celebration of baptism. And within these communal gatherings, the "full, conscious, and active participation called for by the very nature of the liturgy . . . is the aim to be considered before all else" (CSL, 14). In other words, there should be no difference in the quality of the celebration of baptism, whether it is celebrated within Mass or outside Mass.

When baptism is not celebrated within Mass, the presence of the faithful and their full, conscious and active participation in the celebration is still the norm. It is expected that the faithful will participate in song: entrance hymn, responsorial psalm, psalms or songs during the processions, acclamations, baptismal song, Lord's Prayer and hymn after the blessing. It is expected that liturgical ministers will fulfill their ministerial functions as reader, psalmist, cantor, altar server, greeter, musicians, choir, deacon, priest. It is expected that parents and godparents will be prepared to have an active role in the celebration of the baptism of the children. And it is expected that careful attention will be given to the primary symbols and gestures of the rite: the signing with the cross, the anointings with oil, the immersion into the water, the clothing with the white garment, the passing of the light, and the wonderful processions that embody the conversion journey of the baptized. Unless this happens, we will continue to celebrate baptism for children who have not reached catechetical age with privatized notions of church and sacrament.

Conclusion

This brings full circle our discussion of when to celebrate baptism. The goal of liturgical renewal, inaugurated by the Second Vatican Council, can never be fully achieved with just the perfunctory implementation of the revised rites. Nor can it be achieved when the revised rites continue to be celebrated with privatized notions of church and sacrament.

In the case of baptism, the issue of when it is celebrated is an important one because it pertains to the very nature and identity of the sacrament. This is apparent in the implementation of the *Rite of Christian Initiation of Adults,* for which the normal practice in our country is the full initiation of the elect at the Easter Vigil. The profound impact this has on our parish communities is unparalleled. The intimate connection between the liturgical year and the catechumenate is achieved when the elect, having prepared for the celebration of the paschal mystery in union with the local community during the lenten season, are brought to full initiation at the Easter Vigil (RCIA, 206-207).

Consequently *when* we celebrate baptism for children who have not reached catechetical age should be just as important for us as *when* we celebrate the baptism of all persons who are of catechetical age and older so that the meaning of the sacrament can be fully appropriated by all the faithful. The *Rite of Baptism for Children* clearly sets forth preferred times and seasons for the celebration of the sacrament. It also allows for the celebration of baptism outside these times. Given the intimate connection between liturgical time and the nature of the sacrament, however, can we afford not to strive to implement norms that respect the nature of the sacrament and the times for its celebration?

65

Endnotes

1. E.C. Whitaker, *Documents of the Baptismal Liturgy,* (London: SPCK, 1970), 228.

2. Whitaker, 225. Translation modified slightly.

3. *Rite of Christian Initiation of Adults* (RCIA), Introduction, 23. See also RCIA, 17, 207; National Statutes, 14, 15, 18 and 34.

4. *Rite of Christian Initiation of Adults,* 304.

5 Ibid., 27.

6. *Rite of Baptism for Children* (RBC), 9: "To bring out the paschal character of baptism, it is recommended that the sacrament be celebrated during the Easter Vigil or on Sunday, when the church commemorates the Lord's resurrection"; and RBC, 32: "If possible, baptism should take place on Sunday, the day on which the church celebrates the paschal mystery."

The Ministers of the Baptismal Liturgy

Mary Alice Roth, Angie Fagarason, Deanne Tumpich

Saint Julie Billiart parish in Tinley Park, Illinois, is a large parish in a suburb of Chicago. We are a rapidly growing community with lots of children, many baptisms and more than 3,500 registered families. Yet when we looked at the way our parish celebrated baptisms on Sunday afternoons, we realized that, except for the presider, our community was not represented at all! We began to ask ourselves who besides the families should be present at baptisms? How is the local church represented?

Great attention is paid to liturgy at Saint Julie's, but the celebration of the sacrament of baptism was not consistent with the way we did other things. To remedy this, a task force which included our parish priests and deacons, members of the liturgy committee and representatives of the assembly was formed to study the rite and to suggest ways that we might tend to the celebration of baptism with as much care as we gave the Sunday eucharists. As a result of the work of the task force, we modified the way we celebrate baptism in several ways.

Making Changes

The most important change we made in the way we celebrated baptism was to include the full range of liturgical ministers. We felt that through the involvement of various liturgical ministries, our community could be better represented and we could more properly welcome our newest members. When we first asked people who were already serving in the various ministries to extend their service to the celebrations of baptism, there was a willingness and even an enthusiasm to take part. Among the first ministers to volunteer were parents whose children had been baptized at Saint Julie's and who knew that the ritual could and should be celebrated better.

Greeters

The celebration of their child's baptism should be a welcoming and community-building experience for parents. Therefore we determined that the role of the greeter was very important. The first people that families encounter when they arrive for baptism are our greeters, who usually work in pairs. At the time we made the changes in our baptisms, we already had greeters at all our other liturgies. Our first greeters for baptism came from their ranks. Just as friendly people were sought to be greeters at weekend liturgies, friendliness along with organization were the qualities we looked for when recruiting baptism greeters.

67

Our greeters have many responsibilities. Because we want to make sure that the space is ready for the families, our greeters arrive about 45 minutes before the ceremony begins. They check to make sure that everything — including the chairs and the paschal candle — is positioned properly. They reserve seats for the parents and godparents, distribute the worship aids and prepare name tags for the parents.

The most important part of the greeters' job is to make the parents feel comfortable and cared for. The parents and godparents are asked to arrive 30 minutes before the service, and the greeters gather them together to review the service and point out responses in the worship aid. This helps everyone participate in the service more easily. When it is time to begin the celebration, the greeters help the parents and godparents form a procession to the door of the church, where the celebration begins.

Music

Music has long been an integral part of all our other parish sacramental celebrations. We knew that the addition of music to the celebration of baptism would add to the joyfulness of the occasion as well as to the prayerfulness of the community. Rather than training cantors who would serve only at baptisms, we sought out cantors who were already familiar to the parish and who would be willing to serve at these celebrations also. A parish cantor and an accompanist are present at all our baptisms. Together they invite the gathered community to participate as fully as possible.

For each celebration of baptism we prepare a worship aid with the order of service and the necessary songs, refrains and acclamations as well as the babies' and parents' names and some reflection on the symbols used in the celebration. These worship aids also serve as a memento of the event.

Music is part of each element of the rite. When the presider and assembly gather at the door of the church, the cantor is there, too. A simple refrain is sung while the procession moves from the entrance of the church into the main worship space. Once all are at their places, a hymn of praise is sung. The cantor also chants the general intercessions. And after each of the babies is baptized, the parents and the godparents remain at the font while the assembly welcomes its newest member by singing a joyful Alleluia acclamation. To conclude, all are invited to sing a refrain of thanks and praise.

Movement

For the past several years we have used liturgical dancers for our special occasions. At Saint Julie's, dancers are not thought of as "add ons" to the celebration. Rather, they enhance those parts of the liturgy that involve movement, such as the processions, the movement of individuals to and from various places in the church, and the presentation of objects. They raise these from merely practical actions to gracious ritual acts. Two dancers serve at each baptism. They are part of the entrance procession, they present the various symbols (e.g., candles, oil) at the appropriate times, and they escort the families to the font in turn.

Lectors

Like the other ministers, the lectors for baptisms are the parish's regular ministers. This assures that the proclamation of the word, which is so integral to the celebration of this sacrament, is done in a confident, prepared manner.

Commentators

The other minister that serves at baptism is the commentator. Though we have not used commentators at weekend liturgies for years, we find that this role is helpful at baptisms. The commentator welcomes the assembly and then provides occasional commentary throughout the rite. Their words are carefully and poetically scripted and are coordinated with the actions of the rite. Their commentary never overshadows the rite.

Reflections on the Changes

At Saint Julie's, baptisms are celebrated on three Sundays each month. We try to schedule no more than six baptisms at each celebration so that the liturgy is not cumbersome and impersonal.

With six families, however, a large enough assembly is present to celebrate the rites fully.

Because of the number of baptisms, making changes was no small task. But it was certainly worth it. Before we made these changes, there did not seem to be any coherence to the ceremony; it was a series of disjointed rituals. Because each symbol of baptism is now highlighted and connected, the whole assembly is more attentive and prayerful. Families are drawn to participate as a community in the baptism of each baby rather than as individual families interested only in what is happening to their child. The result is a beautiful and prayerful celebration in which a full complement of liturgical ministers represents our parish community in welcoming these newest members of our church.

Grace through Sacramental Signs

David Philippart

I t's more than just the thought that counts. *How* we baptize, *where* we baptize and *what* we use — the sacramental signs — will reveal either God's gracious love or something else. A passive assembly, graceless gestures, a minimum of water, a dab of chrism — all reveal that we don't believe this child is important, this baptism is significant, or this community is worthy of the effort that a fuller celebration requires. It's the difference between a peck on the cheek and a kiss on the lips. No pecks, please! God has acted so generously toward us. Dare we be stingy with the signs of divine love? Dare we skimp when it comes to the signs that save us? A good celebration of baptism requires the full use of its sacramental signs, including the church's house.

Water
The water of baptism is the primordial chaos over which God hovered and brooded before giving birth to life. The water of baptism is the flood that both washed the world of wickedness and

carried the ark to safety. The water of baptism is the whirling Red Sea, parted for Israel's safe passage, that became a torrent crushing Pharaoh's military might. The water of baptism flowed from rocks in the desert and (after the blood) from Jesus' pierced side. The water of baptism is the River Jordan, the river that must be crossed to reach the promised land, the river into which Jesus descended, hallowing all rivers, all water, for all time.

We need this water to baptize: plentiful, clean, reverently contained in a worthy font, carefully and lavishly poured with a seashell or another beautiful vessel. We need to let the water speak for itself: Three dribbles of water hardly proclaim the washing away of the sin of Adam and Eve, the drowning and burial of the sinful self, the birth and rising of a holy one, the grafting of a branch onto the vine, newness of life both individual and communal. We need to baptize by immersion. If the font (or our attitude) makes that seem impossible, then the font (or our attitude) needs to be renovated.

72

Oils

Slathering from head to toe, so slippery as to pop right out of evil's clutches, soothing the skin chafed from being born and bathed, perfuming the head of one destined for God, shining the body of one charged to be the world's light, empowering one called to serve the poor — we need the oil of catechumens and the sacred chrism to initiate and to consecrate Christians, other Christs, followers of the Anointed One and members of Christ's body. We need to let the oils speak for themselves: by using them lovingly and lavishly, by reverently reserving them in worthy vessels more beautiful than brandy decanters. It may be a bit impractical to pour oil over the head of a squirming infant — which means that we need more oil and more time to rub it in. But if we do so, the grace of baptism will be as impossible to ignore as a glistening, sweet-smelling baby: delightful to the eye, smooth to the touch, detected by the nose. Animals know their young by smell. So too with us: Mother Church knows her newborns because they smell like Christ, like chrism, like glory.

Fire

The flame of the paschal candle is shared among the baptized, divided but undimmed by the sharing. In fact, by sharing the flame, by dividing it, the light grows stronger, brighter. Christ is embodied by the paschal candle, Christians by their baptismal candles. Something more than a taper is required. Provide a substantial candle, one that is *at least* one inch in diameter and ten inches tall. Make sure that the candle contains at least some beeswax, for the smell. Some parishes decorate baptismal candles. Although that is not necessary, it can be a nice touch. But instead of using additional symbols (waves, the font or a chi-rho), why not take a cue from the paschal candle's decoration (the cross, the numbers of the year, the five wounds of Christ's passion, the alpha and the omega). It is preferable that the candle remain lit until the end of the rite; therefore, a base should be provided so the candle can be set down if necessary. (Does it make sense to entrust the light of Christ to the godparents and then a few minutes later instruct them to blow it out?) The base will also allow the family to enshrine the candle at home and burn it on the child's birthday, name day and anniversary of baptism each year.

73

Robes

Can a polyester bib with a red chi-rho stitched onto it honestly and powerfully reveal that this child is clothed in Christ? Does it make sense to ask parents to put a bib over the beautifully flowing white gown in which the child is already dressed? Perhaps the easiest way to allow the symbol of the white garment to be full of grace is to let families use their own. Some families have baptismal gowns that have been passed down from generation to generation. Others may procure one for a first child that will then be passed down. Why not use these? Instruct parents to dress the infant in other clothes for the trip to church and to bring the baptismal gown with them, so they can dress the child in it after the water bath.

But be careful with this practice! Don't allow the baptismal gown to become a status symbol, a countersign that distinguishes the babies of the rich, dressed more finely, from the babies of the poor. Always have a few beautiful gowns available for families who may not have them or cannot afford them. Discreetly make them available during the preparation sessions. Or perhaps families in the parish may want to donate gowns, "adopting" a newborn parishioner.

Ministers should wear albs — their own baptismal garments. In addition to alb and stole, the presider could wear a cope. It speaks of the solemnity of the occasion and is easily removed if the presider enters the font with the child. When baptism is celebrated during Mass, the priest changes into a chasuble while the children are being dried and dressed.

The Places of Baptism

The baptismal liturgy is a procession; it is not meant to be a stage play that unfolds in the sanctuary in front of a static audience. The *Rite of Baptism for Children* calls for the liturgy to begin at the door, proceed to the ambo (and the people's seats), then move to the font and finish at the altar (eucharist is baptism's ultimate destination). Something significant is lost when the families are unceremoniously herded into pews until the water bath. Do whatever it takes to celebrate the parts of the rite in their proper places. (In some cases, this may mean studying the necessary church documents and renovating the church building.)

At the Door

Baptism begins at the door because Jesus said "I am the gate to the sheepfold" and because baptism is the door to the sacramental life. Make the narthex or vestibule hospitable so that people can gather and linger there until the rite begins: Clean it, remove unnecessary clutter, provide a few seats for those who need them and set up a diaper-changing table if the restrooms are not nearby. (Perhaps only the families and friends of the children to be baptized will fit in the narthex or vestibule.) Think about decorating the doorway with bunting or garlands of seasonal greenery and flowers. Hang a laurel wreath (a sign of victory — in this case, the victory of Christ over death) on the door as a festive sign of welcome. Such decorations tell the neighborhood (and the assembly) that something special is happening that day, and they make a fitting environment for the opening rites.

At the Ambo

Have candles burning near the ambo, especially when baptism is celebrated outside Mass. Perhaps the paschal candle alone stands burning at the ambo and is then carried to lead the procession to the font. (But then another stand is needed there — a large candle is too heavy to hold for an extended time. And moving furniture during the rite is not a good idea.) Perhaps flowers or a laurel wreath (like the one on the door) could adorn the front of the ambo too, but only if this can be done gracefully, without making the ambo seem like a prop for decoration. Make sure that the readers use the lectionary, and consider using incense at the reading of the gospel.

At the Font

Depending on the design of the font, it too may be adorned with a laurel wreath or flowers. But these must not prevent people from gathering around the font, nor must they prevent the use of copious amounts of water. If the font is in a separate room, garlands might be hung on the walls or tapestries hung from the ceiling.

Also, the ambry (the box holding the holy oils) might be decorated. But more important than any secondary decoration is to have the oils in beautiful vessels (in proper scale to the size of the room).

If the font is not large enough for immersing the child, perhaps a larger vessel can be set up in conjunction with the font. It is important to treat the font with reverence. If an auxiliary vessel or a temporary font is employed, make sure it complements the font's style and decoration. For example, if you have a pedestal font that is too shallow for a child to sit in, find a complementary basin and set it on the floor, off to the side of the font. Put water in both the font and the basin, set the child in the basin and scoop water out of the font to pour over the child.

A towel will be needed to receive the wet child from the font, and another to help dry the child before clothing him or her. Hospitality suggests that these towels be clean, ample and soft.

Set up a corner of the baptistry or, if it is nearby, the sacristy, restroom or bride's room so that the child can be dried and clothed after the water bath. A countertop or changing table and extra towels would be helpful. Parents can be invited to store diaper bags and clothes there before the rite begins. Until the moment of baptism, the child is dressed only in a diaper (which is removed just before putting the child in the font) and wrapped in a blanket. A discreet receptacle for the diaper might be placed near (but not too near) the font.

Unlock the ambry and make sure that the chrism is accessible. (The anointing with the oil of catechumens might be done before coming to the font; if so, that oil may need to be in place elsewhere.) If the chrism is stored elsewhere, a pedestal should be set up for it, or a minister should be designated to carry and hold it. In either case, the chrism should be treated reverently.

At the Altar

When baptism is celebrated at Mass, the liturgy of the eucharist proceeds as usual following the baptism. When baptism is done

apart from Mass, all process to the altar for the Lord's Prayer
and closing rites. When the eucharist is not celebrated, it is best not
to have lighted candles by the altar. The paschal candle might
be used to lead the assembly from font to altar; in that case, it is held
by the minister until the dismissal. The only other candles used
should be those presented to the children and held by their godparents. The altar need not be clothed if eucharist is not celebrated.
Gather the assembly around the altar as much as the space
will allow, and do not set books, papers, towels, candles, blankets
(or babies!) on the Lord's table.

A Homily
for the Baptism of Children

David Philippart

We know what we need to do today. Just like when the pains of labor came upon them and each of these mothers knew what she had to do, we know. Just like each of these fathers knew what he had to do when he first learned that he was going to have a baby, we know. (Just like when these parents received the call that there was a child waiting to be adopted into their hearts, we know.) We who surround these newborns now, we know what we need to do: We need to baptize. We need to immerse these little ones in the faith, in the grace, in the life of the One who loved them before time began, who loves them still, who will love them forever.

So we bring these children here, to the house of the church. Perhaps we bring them here out of superstition: If we don't baptize them, something bad may happen. Perhaps we bring them here out of a sense of tradition: You have a baby, you have a baptism. Perhaps we bring them here out of hope, hope that their lives will be as good as, if not better than, our own. Perhaps we bring them here out of faith, out of a strong belief that the gospel is eternal life, and that to immerse these children into Jesus' dying and rising is to open up for them the possibility of life everlasting. Perhaps we bring them here for a combination of these reasons. But one thing is certain: We bring them here mostly out of love: out of love for them, out of love for God, out of the love that is God.

Our motives for doing this baptism are wonderfully mixed. But what is the significance of what we are doing? What does this thing that we know we must do — this baptism — mean? What sense does it make in this modern day and this scientific era to say that this sacrament of baptism brings to birth new and eternal life? Why, in light of this wonderful mystery, faced with these lovely, tiny creatures who are so dependent on us and yet so new and strange, do we bathe and anoint them? The meaning is found in the doing. What are we doing?

Some Christians don't baptize babies. Aware — as we must also be — that baptism into Christ is death to self in order to live for God, some communities insist that baptism is a commitment that only adults can make. They are correct: Baptism is an adult commitment. But it doesn't necessarily follow that we shouldn't baptize babies. For baptism is not only a commitment that we make to God, not only something that we do; it is also (primarily) something that God does, a commitment that God makes to us. And while we marvel at these tiny creatures, wondering what they are thinking and experiencing, completely amazed at how helpless they are, we know that in their own mysterious way they are aware of God. And we know that God relates to them now in ways we cannot perceive. The psalmist knew this. Perhaps the words of Psalm 139 articulate the experiences of these babies: Years from now, when these children can talk and sing, they will sing to God these words and know them to be true:

> You created every part of me,
> knitting me in my mother's womb.
> For such handiwork, I praise you.
> Awesome this great wonder!

And so it is this wondrous, mysterious relationship that these newborns have with God that leads us to baptize them. God is present to these newborns, and they are present to God.

What about us, then? Where do we come in? Just as we must care for the physical needs of these helpless little ones, so too we must tend their relationship with God. We must support it and nourish it. It is a living thing. That's the commitment that we are making today—the commitment that we make to these children and to God. For if, as the African proverb says, it takes a whole village to raise a child, then it follows that it takes a whole church to make a Christian. We pledge ourselves to walk with these children as they learn to walk with God.

That's why we met them at the door. We met them while they were still outside so that we could carry them inside. The parents spoke their children's names aloud for the first time in this church and requested, on their behalf, entrance into this assembly. And then we walked them to this ambo to hear the word of God. Of course, they may not understand it yet in the ways that we understand it, but they have heard it nonetheless, washed, as it were, in these words of scripture.

Next we will walk them to the font, calling out the names of the saints as we go, evoking the memories and invoking the help of our ancestors who walked this way before us, the tribe into which these children are being accepted. The paschal candle will lead them there, the pillar of fire that led Israel on its exodus away from the evil machinations of worldly wealth and power, epitomized in Pharaoh's Egypt. And at the font we will immerse them in the water, washing off the image of Adam and Eve to reveal in them the image of Christ.

We will immerse them in this water, the waters that seethed with chaos before the earth was born, the waters over which the Holy Spirit brooded like a hen warming her eggs. We will put them in this water, the water of the flood that drowned sinfulness to death but carried Noah and his wife and pairs of all living creatures to

safety. We will splash them with this water, the water that
flowed from rocks in the desert. We will lead them through this water,
the waters of the Red Sea that separated sluggish slavery from
sojourn, the waters of the River Jordan that separated the desert
of aimless wandering from the destination of life with God in the
promised land. We will wash them in this water, the water that
flowed from the pierced side of the Savior who loved us to the death.
Reborn from these waters, these children claim all of history as
their own story and salvation as their destiny.

And because these waters are as dangerous as they are
delightful, as death-dealing to the Adam and Eve in us as they are
life-giving to the Christ in us, before we dare put these little ones in
these waters, we will slather them with the oil of catechumens.
Oil and water don't mix. So, slippery with the Spirit's balm, these
young ones will not drown in these waters but will be safely carried
by them to the other side to live forever.

81

And when we have thus bathed them, we will anoint them
again but with the perfumed oil of prophets, priests and sovereigns.
We will anoint them with sacred chrism and make them other
Christs — anointed ones, set apart for God, empowered with the
Holy Spirit, rubbed through and through with wisdom, grace and
love. And we will robe them in new clothes and give them a burning
candle. Listen to what is said when we give this gift to the
godparents to hold, for the words that we speak explain our
commitment to these children before God: "This light is entrusted to
you to be kept burning brightly. This child has been enlightened by
Christ and is to walk always as a child of the light."

Walk always as a child of the light. But because they are not
yet able to walk, we will carry these little ones to the altar and pray
the Lord's Prayer with them. Unable yet to share in the paschal
banquet, they are destined to do so. Baptism guarantees them a seat
at the Lord's table, so we carry them there as a pledge on our part
to do everything and anything that it will take, these next few
years, to help them walk to this table on their own two feet, to come

in here bearing the bread and wine of their young lives as an offering to God, an offering that will be consecrated and changed into the body and blood of Christ, and returned to us as the bread of life and the cup of salvation.

Finally, we carry them from this altar back outside, back to the world—the world that they enter for the first time as Christians, the world to which they will pledge their lives, to serve in Christ's name, the world that they will change as they grow in holiness and gradually take up the mission of the gospel, loving others, loving God.

Are we ready? Are we ready to walk this way for and with these children? We must pause and think about it. The few steps that we have already taken this day—from door to ambo—and the few steps that we will take next—from ambo to font, to altar, to world—are life-changing steps. Are we ready? Are we willing to believe so strongly that our faith washes over these little ones and carries them along with it? Are we willing to walk the way of sacrificial love, the path that says, "I will give my life so that you may live," the way of the cross? Are we willing to make our way to the tomb, and when we find it empty, to run to Jerusalem, to the world, with the news? Are we willing to do this with these children? For them? Now? If so, come on. Let's do what we know we must do.

Baptismal Preparation: How One Parish Does It

James S. Musumeci

Baptismal preparation programs come in all shapes and sizes. Each parish needs to construct its own program, taking into account the elements discussed throughout this book and the unique character of the people and leadership of the community.

In the program of preparation and pastoral care that we developed for families preparing to celebrate the baptism of an infant at Saint Laurence parish in Brooklyn, New York, there are five major elements: pastoral involvement, instruction, community participation, liturgical celebration and follow-up. These elements are combined in various ways in the many components that make up this program: the interview, the evening of awareness, Presentation Sunday, registration, the evenings of instruction, the celebration of baptism and the follow-up program. In this chapter I will describe each of these components and offer some suggestions about how they might be implemented.

Interview

When a parent or parents who wish to have their child baptized call the parish office, an appointment with a member of the parish staff is arranged. This interview is one of the most important phases of our program. The staff member who meets with the parents strives to be welcoming, attentive, patient and friendly. For many parents, this interview may be their first impression of the parish; the tone that is set here will remain with the parents throughout and beyond the process of preparation for baptism.

The staff person who interviews the parents will be their main contact with the parish throughout the process that leads to baptism and beyond. It is this person's responsibility to determine the suitable path for each couple (in the case of unmarried parents, we try, if at all possible, to involve both parents) and, in consultation with others, to make the final pastoral decision concerning the baptism.

At the initial interview, basic information such as the child's name and the names of the parents, their religion, marital status, address and telephone number are obtained and placed on file. The main purpose of the interview, however, is to begin for the parents a time of awareness and preparation so that when their child is baptized, it may also be an event that celebrates their own faith.

The discussion during this interview focuses on the parents' relationship to the child, on the parents' own faith and on their reasons for requesting baptism for their child. This should be done in a friendly, relaxed way. After listening to the parents, the interviewer might invite the parents to what we call an "evening of awareness," suggest that the parents meet with the same interviewer again, or arrange for a special program of instruction for the parents, depending on what best suits their needs. In any case, a definite date for the baptism of the child is not set at this time.

Invitation to the Evening of Awareness

Parents who have a general awareness of their faith, who gather with the community regularly for worship and who proclaim faith in

Jesus by their work and action are given a letter of invitation to the next evening of awareness (The sample letter on the next page is suited to one particular pastoral situation. Each parish's will, of course, be different.). This evening, which will be described more fully later, is designed to give parents the tools with which to make an informed decision or, in the case of the faith-filled parents, to give them time to reinforce and strengthen their decision to have their child baptized.

Personal Follow-up

Parents who have recently moved into the parish, lapsed Catholics who are searching for a place of worship or those who are uncomfortable with "church" might be best helped through a personal follow-up rather than the evening of awareness at this time. The interviewer might offer to meet with the parents again about a month after the initial interview and after the parents have had the opportunity to attend Sunday Mass and to get to know the parish a little better.

At the second interview they could then discuss their relationship to the parish. For example, are they comfortable praying with the people of this parish? Is this the parish they wish to worship with regularly? At the end of the interview, the staff member might invite the parents to attend the evening of awareness or a special instruction program, or he or she might suggest that they continue to meet with the staff person.

Special Instruction Program

Parents who are uncatechized or who have serious questions or confusions about the church, their faith or baptism may choose to take part in a special instruction program that can be arranged for them. The program would provide very basic instruction on God, faith and the church. In some cases this program might parallel the Christian initiation process or be an invitation to be part of the catechumenate journey. At any time that seems appropriate, the parents can be invited to an evening of awareness.

85

Letter of Invitation to the Evening of Awareness

Dear Parents,

Congratulations on the birth (adoption) of your child! We join with your family in thanking God for this gift of life. You have asked that your child be baptized and become a member of God's church and family. It is a very joyful experience for us to welcome a new Christian into the church and into our parish community.

Baptism is a sacrament of faith. As parents, it is your faith and that of the whole community that gives meaning to the celebration of this sacrament for your child. In our parish, we have a program of preparation and follow-up to explain the meaning and celebration of baptism and to help you as parents create a Christian environment for your child during his or her preschool years.

To begin your preparation for your child's baptism, you are invited to the next introductory session of our program, "An Evening of Awareness," which will be held on [date] in [place]. Together we will focus on the meaning of faith and the effect faith has on our lives.

Because we consider this session to be very important, and because we wish to respect both your time and ours, we ask that you be on time.

- We will welcome you beginning at 7:45 PM.
- If you cannot make it by 8:00, please attend next month's session, which will be held on [date].
- We ask that both parents attend.
- We regret that we are not able to provide child care. Please arrange for your children to be cared for at home.
- We will end promptly at 9:30 PM.

Further information about the program of preparation will be given to you at this session.

Know that the prayers of the parish community are with you during this important time of preparation.

In Christ,

The Baptismal Team

Evening of Awareness

The purpose of this evening is to help parents become more aware of their faith, its implications and its demands. For those parents who have not yet made a firm decision, it will enable them to make an informed decision concerning the baptism of their child. We believe it is very important that both parents attend.

Outline of Evening of Awareness

WELCOME AND INTRODUCTION (10 minutes)
Welcome
Introduction of team
Purpose of evening
What we will do

FIRST DISCUSSION GROUP (15 minutes)
Ice-breaker, reduce apprehension, clarify expectations

FOLLOWING JESUS (15 minutes)
A theological talk on the faith life to which we are called

HOW WE LIVE OUT THIS FAITH LIFE (10 minutes)
A witness talk of how ordinary Christians try to do this

SECOND DISCUSSION GROUP (20 minutes)
A time to assimilate what was presented
and how it affects our faith and life

CLOSING REMARKS: THE DECISION (15 minutes)
The rich young man's decision; your decision

The evening of awareness is a 90-minute session that consists of both talks and discussion on the theme of following Jesus. The evening begins with a welcome given by a married couple. After a period of discussion to break the ice and give everyone a chance to say what they are looking for and to hear what others have to say, a parish staff member offers a theological reflection on the life of faith. Another married couple then witnesses to how they try to live this out in their daily lives. A discussion follows to help parents assimilate some of the ideas presented. The evening concludes with closing remarks by a parish staff member. These remarks focus on the gospel story of the rich young man.

As the parents leave, they are given a pamphlet containing the story of the rich young man (Mark 10:17 – 31) and some thoughts on their decision in faith to have their child baptized. They also receive a copy of the Presentation Sunday ceremony. The parents are asked to discuss at home if they are ready to profess their faith and if they want their child baptized. If they are, they are asked to call the parish office the following Saturday morning and leave a message for the appropriate person.

The Saturday Phone Call

At the evening of awareness, parents are asked to call the parish office and inform us if they wish to have their child baptized. If they call, they will be reminded to attend a specific liturgy the following Sunday, at which time they will ask the community to pray for them and their child as they prepare for the child's baptism. They will also be informed about registration and asked to bring the child's birth certificate to the liturgy.

Presentation Sunday

The parents have a right to the support and encouragement of the community, and the community has a right to know the intention and commitment of the parents who present their child for baptism. This short presentation ceremony takes place after the homily at a different Sunday Mass each month. The presider asks the parents if they believe and practice the faith of the church and intend to raise their children in the faith. The parents ask for baptism for their child, and the community, in turn, prays that God will bless and strengthen these parents. Following the liturgy, a formal registration of the child to be baptized takes place.

Registration

Registration for baptism takes place immediately after the Mass at which the presentation ceremony took place. The information needed for the church records is taken at this time. Parents are asked to bring the child's birth certificate with them so that a reference to the certificate can be made in the baptismal records. A booklet on baptism (several of the pamphlets in LTP's *Baptism Is a Beginning* series would be ideal) and an information letter about the evenings of instruction and the celebration of baptism are given to the parents. At this time, a definite date is set for the baptism.

Letter of Invitation for the Evenings of Instruction

Dear Parents,

You have asked to have your child baptized. You have proclaimed before the entire community that your faith makes you ready to accept the responsibility of training your child in the practice of the faith. It will be your duty, with the help of the godparents you have chosen and the whole Christian community, to bring up your child to keep God's commandments as Christ taught us, by loving God and our neighbor.

To help you prepare for the celebration of baptism, we invite you to two Evenings of Instruction, which will be held at [place] on [date] and [date]. At that time we will focus together on the meaning of baptism — what it is, how we live it, and how we celebrate it.

Because of the importance of the evening, we ask that you be on time.

- We will welcome you beginning at 7:30 PM.
- We will begin the program at 7:45 PM and end at 9:45 PM.
- We ask that both parents and both godparents attend.
- We regret that we are not able to provide child care. Please arrange for your children to be cared for at home.

Please read the enclosed booklet on baptism before the first evening of instruction. We know you will find it very helpful.

A reminder: The celebration of baptism will take place on Sunday, [date] at the 2:00 PM Mass. Parents, child and godparents are asked to be in the church by 1:45 PM.

Know that our prayers are with you in these remaining days before your child's baptism.

In Christ,

The Baptismal Team

Team Phone Call

Several days before the first instruction session, parents receive a call from one of the team couples reminding them about the evening of instruction.

Evenings of Instruction

These two evenings of instruction focus on baptism, what it is and how we, as church, celebrate it. The speakers emphasize how family life reflects Christian values and prayer. Both parents and both godparents are asked to attend, unless extraordinary situations prevent them.

Several challenges are presented to parents to engage their hearts and their faith toward growth and understanding. We take seriously the guidelines of our diocese, the diocese of Brooklyn, which say in part,

> Unless parents, on the occasion of their child's baptism, experience through their own lives a renewal of what baptism means in terms of commitment to a Christian community and a way of life, the whole celebration is ineffective.

91

These two evenings, like the evening of awareness, are a blend of brief presentations and discussion. The presentations focus on helping the parents and godparents understand what sacraments are, particularly baptism, and how they relate to everyday Christian life, particularly as it is lived in the family environment. Some time also is spent on the rituals and symbols of the celebration of baptism, but care is taken not to "explain away" the mystery. Periods of discussion allow the parents to respond to the process of preparation that they have experienced so far and to share with other parents and godparents on the topics of the presentation.

At the end of the second evening, parents and godparents are asked to evaluate the process of preparation they have just completed. Reminders about the time of baptism are given and a final check is made that all the information needed is complete and correct.

Celebration of Baptism

We celebrate baptism on one Sunday every month, except during Lent, during a special eucharist at 2:00 PM. We have found that a consistent schedule throughout the year — for example, the fourth Sunday of every month in English, the second Sunday of every other month in Spanish — works best in our situation.

We ask that the child, parents and godparents be in the church at least 15 minutes before Mass begins. Family and friends are encouraged to gather together in prayer at this time.

Even though this liturgy is not one of the usual Sunday Masses, all the principles of good liturgy are followed. The assembly is invited and supported to participate fully. A special worship aid is prepared to encourage participation and to serve as a memento of the occasion. A full complement of ministers (lectors, acolytes, musicians, ministers of eucharist, deacon, priest) are present. (See Timothy Fitzgerald, *Infant Baptism: A Parish Celebration* [LTP, 1993] for a complete presentation of the celebration of baptism. The video *New Life: A Parish Celebrates Infant Baptism* [a joint project of LTP and Tabor Publishing Company, 1996] offers a look at the way one parish celebrates and understands infant baptism.)

Follow-up

Following up with the parents after the celebration of baptism is an important part of pastoral care, yet it often is ignored or thought to be unimportant. Throughout the program, parents are invited to journey in their faith and to stretch themselves in understanding God. The baptism of the child does not signal the end of this process. Parents must know that the community supports them, remembers them and invites them to join others in prayer and service. The follow-up ideas suggested here are occasional reminders to parents of the prayers and concern of the Christian community. Elsewhere in this book, suggestions for gathering with parents for mystagogical reflection are offered (see chapters 2 and 9).

The Baptismal Certificate

The baptismal certificate is brought to the children's homes within two weeks after the baptism, at a time arranged in advanced. The home visit provides a pastoral opportunity to strengthen the parish's relationship with the family and to let the parents know that the parish is ready to assist the parents in providing an environment for the child to know and worship God.

Reunion Mass

Twice a year we invite all parents who have had children baptized in the preceding six months to a particular Sunday eucharist. It is an opportunity for parents to meet one another and for the congregation to congratulate and show its support of the parents and children who have been baptized.

Anniversary Card

An anniversary card is sent to parents one year after the date of the baptism. It is a small way of keeping in touch with them and offering them continued support and encouragement for living a Christian life. Further contact may be maintained for a longer period of time by sending articles or other materials at various intervals. For example, LTP's *Baptism Is a Beginning* includes several pamphlets appropriate for this purpose.

Reflections on This Program

The baptism preparation outlined here is the result of teamwork among a group of priests, religious women and dedicated laity, including Theresa Agliardi, RSM, Maryann and Jim Kimball, Ann and Ozzie Ramos, Rosemarie and Richard Savarino, Winston and Helen Sealy, Isaac and Carmen Torres, and Al and Kathy VanHolt.

This program is also accompanied by an extensive training program for the various ministers who lead this process. Training includes reflection on the ministers' own relationship to Christ and to the church, some instruction on the church's theology of the sacraments of marriage and baptism, training in group dynamics and facilitation, and extensive work on the writing and delivery of their presentations. All of this is done in an atmosphere of respect and faith.

There is no instant formula for a program that will work in any given environment. Those with the pastoral responsibility of meeting people's spiritual needs are constantly challenged to assess the situation, develop a rationale and design for the program, train leaders and assistants, implement the plan and put in place support systems for the continued development of the leaders and the evaluation of the program.

This program developed over a period of several years. At first, parents were asked to reflect on their own understanding of baptism and their request for their child's baptism. If their faith made them ready to accept this responsibility, they were asked to bring their child to the baptism liturgy — two days later. Hardly an opportunity for reflection! By that time, family arrangements were made and the expectation was that the child would be baptized on Sunday.

An additional evening was added to slow what we termed the "steamroller effect." The interview process gave no baptism date, and no date was set until "Presentation Sunday." Most, though not all, parents completed the program. Unfortunately, we had no further contact with those who dropped out.

About half the parents who did have their children baptized were seldom seen again. Their comments about the program, however, were quite positive. They had a good experience with a church that did not give up on them. We were gentle yet firm in our requirements, and not overly demanding or harsh.

About 15 percent of the parents returned to weekly worship with the community. Their experience of the program invited them back. We were able to strike a chord that resonated with them, and it was good to see them.

The regular churchgoers were at first mystified and sometimes annoyed at the instruction program. "Why must a faithful member be penalized?" Some were so spiritually moved by the program, however, that they became members of the team.

All these experiences helped shape and direct the baptism program. It was a program that became stronger because of the contributions of each team member and the comments from the participants, and it was a program that remained focused on the needs of the parents.

Developing a Program

The ideas in this chapter are not meant to be a blueprint for anyone. This is a model developed for a specific place. Use the ideas to develop your own program. Gather a group of people to review this and other models and to dream about "what could be" in your own situation. Begin by exploring the following areas:

1. *Purpose:* What do you hope the program will accomplish? What changes do you hope will occur in people as a result of their participation?

2. *Participation:* Who will take part? What parish ministers will collaborate (e.g., priest, deacon, pastoral associate, catechetical leaders)? What new ministries will need to be developed (e.g., sponsor couples, team members)?

3. *Content:* Given your purpose, what specific areas do you want to touch on in the program? What will be emphasized? What topics will be addressed?

4. *Contact with parents:* What kinds of meetings will be required? How will individual contact be handled?

5. *Community needs:* How will you take into account the needs of your specific community? What cultural circumstances need to be considered? What parish customs need to respected? What other concerns (e.g., security for evening meetings, child care, meeting spaces) need to be considered?

6. *Liturgical needs:* When is the best time to celebrate the sacrament of baptism? During Mass? On a Sunday afternoon? How will the people of the parish be invited and encouraged to participate in the baptismal liturgy and be engaged with the families who are presenting their children for baptism?

These are only a few of the things that need to be considered. Guidance on these and other issues is offered throughout this book. Give the planning of this important part of parish life all the time it needs. Remember that evaluation and fine-tuning are ongoing aspects of the program. And allow the Spirit of God to energize you, stir your imagination and shape your creativity.

Mystagogy: Ministry to Parents

Catherine Dooley

The revised rite of infant baptism offers a great opportunity for parish renewal and for ministering to parents of young children. The theology of the revised initiation rites, both the *Rite of Baptism for Children* (RBC) and the *Rite of Christian Initiation of Adults,* calls for a major shift in the approach to initiation. In both infant baptism and the Christian initiation process accommodated to children of catechetical age (usually seven years or older), the primary focus is not on the readiness of the infant or child but on the readiness of the community as a whole, represented concretely by parents, sponsors, godparents, catechists and the local community.

The Faith of the Church

Because the sacraments are "sacraments of faith," this shift in approach is best expressed in the ancient phrase "the faith of the church." Just before the parents and godparents profess their faith at the baptism of an infant, the presider says to them:

> If your faith makes you ready to accept this responsibility, renew now the vows of your own baptism. Reject sin; profess your faith in Christ Jesus. This is the faith of the church. This is the faith in which this child is about to be baptized. (RBC, 56)

The parents and godparents who make this profession of faith are not making promises for the child until the time comes that the child is mature enough to speak for himself or herself. They speak, rather, in their own names and take upon themselves the responsibility of helping the child grow into the Christian life. Believing parents give a definite orientation to the life of their child. They hand on that which they themselves have received. The infant (and the adult catechumen) is baptized in the faith of the church and initiated into that faith. It follows from this that spiritual preparation of the parents, godparents and sponsors and the entire local community is of great importance so that they understand their responsibilities and their commitment to the child.

The "faith of the church" encompasses several levels of meaning. It is that faith which has come to us from the apostles, handed down from generation to generation through the scriptures, liturgy, creedal formulations and the witness of Christian women and men. The faith of the church refers to that universal community of faith, "the common treasure of the whole church of Christ," which is realized in the local church. The faith of the church is constituted by the pattern of dying and rising that is lived out by the community of the baptized. Baptism is the intentional incorporation of the child into an environment of faith, the faith of the church, the faith of Christ himself.

Initiation Is a Gradual Process

The corollary to the emphasis on the faith of the church in the rite of baptism is that initiation is a gradual process in which the sacramental ritual marks but one part of an initiatory process that extends over time. Baptism is not restricted to the moment of celebration but is lived out in the future. The process of formal initiation begins with preparatory catechesis that enables the parents and community to enter into the ritual insightfully. Following the celebration, further catechesis based on the actual celebration itself uncovers those deeper meanings richly inlaid in the sacramental heritage.

What Is Mystagogy?

Mystagogy (a term meaning "initiation into the meaning of the mystery") is the name that the early church gave to this post-baptismal interpretation of the mysteries celebrated on Holy Saturday night. The early mystagogues (catechists and preachers who interpreted the mysteries) understood mystery in a biblical sense, as God's design or what the *Catechism of the Catholic Church* (#50) calls God's "plan of loving goodness" for humanity and for the world. In a sacramental sense, mystery meant baptism and eucharist, the means by which believers were initiated into God's plan of salvation.

The basic principle of mystagogy is pastorally and pedagogically astute: Reflection is drawn out of the experience of the rites. Cyril of Jerusalem, in the fourth century, noted,

> Since seeing is far more persuasive than hearing, I delayed
> until the present occasion, knowing that I would find you
> more open to the influence of my words out of your personal
> experience. (*Mystagogical Catechesis,* I.1)

Through reflection on the prayers and readings and the symbols and rituals of the baptismal liturgy, the newly baptized are able to clarify and extend the meaning of sacramental initiation. In this way they come to a deeper participation in the mystery they have celebrated, and they are prepared to live a life of faithfulness to Christ.

The baptismal liturgy contains the central symbols that are used over and over again in liturgical worship and which proclaim the fundamental Christian story: the gathering of the assembly, immersing in water, anointing with oil, illuminating the darkness, laying on hands, proclaiming the word and professing faith (sharing of bread and wine). These actions and interactions provide a rich mystagogical catechesis for the young child and its parents in the early, formative years.

Infant Baptism and Mystagogy

What does this mean with regard to infant baptism? In most cases, very little time or energy has been given to the faith development of parents in the years between the baptism and first communion of their child. The experience of implementing Christian initiation with adults has brought many catechists to realize that the community's efforts during these years of early childhood — years that psychologists tell us are crucial in the child's religious development — would best focus on mystagogical reflection on the symbols of baptism. The implementation of a mystagogical process for infant baptism will need the cooperation of both catechists and liturgists.

In the Christian initiation of adults, the catechetical sessions during the catechumenate (the prebaptismal period of formation) focus on the readings of the Sunday scripture and integrating them with the Catholic tradition found in the creeds and in the witness of Christian life. The sessions following baptism are not didactic in approach; they do not explain but rather interrelate the images, metaphors and stories that unveil and interpret the significance of the baptismal symbols. The *Rite of Christian Initiation of Adults* intends that this postbaptismal period of initiation, which usually takes place on the Sundays of the fifty days of the Easter season, is valued not only for the insight it holds for the newly baptized but also for the continuing sacramental and theological education it provides the entire local community of believers. The deepest significance of the initiation event is generally not immediately grasped and requires time for integrating and for seeing the connections.

Who Participates?

In some parishes the parents, godparents, sponsors, friends and family of the baptized infant, the newly baptized adults (neophytes) and all in the community who wish to be part of the reflection gather after the Sunday liturgy. If the group is large, it is divided into smaller groups. In other parishes the parents, godparents and sponsors of the infants meet as a separate group in order to focus more specifically on parenting and on questions of raising children in faith.

What about toddlers or very young children? A babysitting service is essential for the participation of parents, but these sessions can be used to introduce young children in very simple words and celebrations to the imagery and liturgical action that is the basis of adult reflection. Children need a wide variety of experiences as currency for future understanding. As a child grows and begins to question, links are made between what has been experienced and what it means in terms of the Christian life. What the child has already intuited through simple prayer celebrations, ritual actions and scriptural stories takes on deeper levels of significance as the child matures.

101

Format for Mystagogical Sessions

The *Rite of Baptism for Children* (#3) states that the foundation of formation in faith is the sacrament itself. The starting point in mystagogy, therefore, is the rite and the community celebrating. The following is one example of how the parents, catechist and/or liturgist might shape a mystagogical session.

As the participants gather, refreshments are available. After the group is called to order, participants and leaders introduce themselves. A reading from the Sunday lectionary or from the rite of baptism is then proclaimed, followed by an opening prayer.

The leader gives a brief introduction to the ritual element, such as the naming of the child, that will be the focus of reflection. For example, the leader reminds the group that in the celebration of baptism the first question parents are asked is: "What name do you give your child?" The naming of a child is awesome; the name that one receives is a name for eternity. *The Catechism of the Catholic Church* reminds us that "God calls each one by name. Everyone's name is sacred. The name is an icon of the person. It demands respect as a sign of the dignity of the one who bears it" (#2158).

In the mystagogical session, the leader asks the parents and members of the community to speak about their own names.

Why were they given the name they have?

What importance do names have for an individual or a community?

In what instances have they been aware of the power of names or of naming?

Why did they choose the name they have given their child?

In giving that name to their child, what was it that they wanted for their child?

The leader can then present several of the passages from scripture that deal with names. As the adults reflect on the meaning of the name in each passage, ask them to relate the scriptural meaning to the baptismal rite. What does this particular understanding of name say about baptism?

Some passages that could be used are:

1) Genesis 17:3–8; 15–16.   God, in the context of the making of the covenant, tells Abram that he will now be called Abraham and that Sarai, his wife, will be called

Sarah. The change of names brings about a new identity in accord with their new task or mission. Being baptized in Christ means becoming a new creation and assuming a new way of acting.

2) Matthew 1:21–23.   Joseph is told that Mary will bear a son who is to be named Jesus, a name which means "The Lord saves" or "savior." "Emmanuel" (v. 23) means "God is with us" and is the short form of the covenant formula, "I am your God and you will be my people."

3) John 20:15–16.   Mary of Magdala mistakes Jesus for the gardener but recognizes him when Jesus calls her name.

Other passages that could be used are 1 Samuel 3 (Samuel, God's gift to Hannah, is called by name and is called to give his life to God); Matthew 16 (Simon is renamed Peter in light of his mission); Acts 9 (Saul after his conversion becomes Paul).

103

The *Catechism of the Catholic Church* has sections on God's name (#203–221), Jesus (#430–451) and names, titles and symbols of the Holy Spirit (#691–701) that may also be sources of reflection.

After relating these scriptural passages to the naming in the baptismal rite, the leader asks the group to think back to the ritual action in which the minister calls the children by name and says that the Christian community welcomes them: "In its name I claim you for Christ our Savior by the sign of the cross." In baptism the child becomes Christian, a name that gives identity and mission.

What does it mean to be Christian?

What does this name ask of us?

The session closes with prayer and ritual. Reading 1 Peter 1:3–9 (a prayer of praise and thanksgiving to God who gives the gift of new life and hope in baptism) or singing Psalm 8 are suggestions for prayer. The group marks each other with sign of the cross, saying, "You have been claimed by Christ by this sign." The leader encourages the parents to sign their children each day at home before the children go to sleep or before they leave the house.

Another session might focus on the blessing and invocation of God over the baptismal water as a way of reflecting on the significance of water in baptism. The blessing is a summary of God's saving action in human history and God's promise of faithful love in the biblical stories that are important foundations to an understanding of sacraments. The biblical stories, with their images of water as the wellspring of all holiness, as new beginning, as freedom from sin, communicate the saving presence of God in the world today. A sprinkling rite with an acclamation (see page 69 in *The Hymnal for Catholic Students* [LTP, 1988] for one suggestion) is an appropriate prayer response.

Any part of the ritual — the proclamation of the word, the anointing, the profession of faith, the baptismal formula, the clothing with the white garment, the lighted candle, the blessing — can be the starting point for mystagogy. The community's reflection on the liturgical action and prayers includes personal response, integration of the scriptures into the framework of the liturgical season, and a challenge to more fully live the Christian life. The appendices to both the *Rite of Baptism for Children* and the *Rite of Christian Initiation of Adults* are valuable resources, providing a wide variety of options for scriptural readings, prayers and responses. The introduction to the rite offers a theology of the sacrament and a context for clarifying doctrinal points.

An ongoing mystagogy supports parents in their striving to hand on their faith. It encourages, supports and brings the realization that the ordinary events of each day are the way in which faith is communicated. Mystagogy can awaken a parish community to its responsibility in handing on the faith of the church, the faith we are proud to profess in Christ Jesus.

BULLETIN INSERTS

WHAT DO YOU ASK OF GOD'S CHURCH?

When children are baptized, the priest or deacon asks the parents, "What do you ask of God's church for your children?" The parents then speak their request for their children: "Baptism," they may say, or "faith," "the grace of Christ," "entrance into the church," "eternal life" or something similar. This response is key to understanding the sacramental life of the church.

Faith is a mystery. In faith we come to believe the deepest truths and to know the ways of God. Entrance into the church is the beginning of the journey of faith. This journey is led by God and is shared with others to whom God has given the gift of faith. The journey may, at times, get lonely and the path may seem unclear, but the traditions and the wisdom of the community of the faithful are maps and signposts on our way to God's reign. Sharing the journey with a new member gives an occasion for more experienced travelers to tell the stories and memories of the journey, to remember the hardships and joys along the way, to realize again the presence of God at every step of the way.

To walk with another on the journey of life and faith is the role of the community and, especially, of the godparents of the newly baptized. Godparents are mentors and guides. They are chosen to assist the parents as they guide their children in the practice of faith. Each member of the community is also a role model, mentor and guide. Even though we personally may not know the one being baptized, we together are the church and are therefore responsible for handing on the stories and the faith of the church. The question that the parents are asked at the beginning of the rite of baptism, "What do you ask of God's church for your children?" means "What do you ask of us?" How will we answer?

Text by Jane Marie Osterholt, SP. Art by Laura Montenegro. Copyright 1996, Archdiocese of Chicago: Liturgy Training Publications, 1800 North Hermitage Avenue, Chicago IL 60622-1101. All rights reserved.

THE CHRISTIAN COMMUNITY
WELCOMES YOU WITH GREAT JOY

*B*aptism is a communal celebration of being welcomed and being plunged into the life of Christ. Welcoming takes on many different forms based on cultural and familial experiences. Most often when we meet someone, we greet that person and introduce ourselves.

As the newest members of this community, of God's church, are baptized, the assembled community is given the opportunity to welcome them with great joy. To greet someone is to recognize God present within that person. The celebration of baptism begins with a welcome ceremony at the entrance of the church. In the name of the community, the priest or deacon asks the name of the one to be baptized. It is the first question asked, so that from then on the child may called by name, treated as an individual and respected as unique and special in God's eyes.

At the conclusion of this brief welcoming, the priest or deacon addresses the child by name and says, "The Christian community welcomes you with great joy." As we come to understand this part of the rite, we take time to reflect on its meaning in our individual lives as well as in the life of the community, the parish assembly. The words "great joy" remind us of the gospel story of the angels appearing to the shepherds to announce the birth of Jesus. Joy should be the characteristic of all Christians, and "great joy" is the hallmark of welcome. Let us greet one another — the newest members and the same old wonderful faces we see each week — with great joy!

WELCOME YOUR CHILDREN
NEWBORN OF WATER

In his ministry among us, Jesus used the ordinary and made it holy. He used touch to heal the sick and to forgive. He made bread and wine his presence among us. He made water the way to be born to new life. Just as we still use touch and bread and wine in Jesus' name, we use water, an element so vital, yet so often taken for granted. The ordinary becomes holy, and we too are made holy. As those to be baptized are immersed in or drenched with this water three times, they are immersed into the Trinity and newborn into the mystery of God.

Sometimes the presence of water frightens or concerns us; we become overwhelmed and forget the saving power of God. Yet through the sign of the cross, the sign of our baptism, we are reminded of the saving power of God, of being born anew in God. Each time we sign ourselves with holy water as we come into or leave a church, or we sign ourselves as we pray, we are reminded of our baptism, of the power of God within us. This simple gesture is filled with a power and beauty that remind us of what it means to be newborn of God. As we sign ourselves with the sign of the cross, may we be reminded of the importance of being signed with the sign of a Christian, the sign of God present in the water of baptism. Let us remember how important it is to welcome all those children, regardless of age, who are newborn of water!

Text by Jane Marie Osterholt, SP. Art by Laura Montenegro. Copyright 1996, Archdiocese of Chicago: Liturgy Training Publications, 1800 North Hermitage Avenue, Chicago IL 60622-1101. All rights reserved.

THE FULLNESS OF GOD'S SPIRIT . . . THE BANQUET OF CHRIST'S SACRIFICE

Before the celebration of infant baptism concludes with the Lord's Prayer, the celebrant says:

> Dearly beloved, these children have been reborn in baptism. They are now called children of God, for so indeed they are. In confirmation they will receive the fullness of God's Spirit. In holy communion they will share the banquet of Christ's sacrifice, calling God their Father in the midst of the church. In their name . . . let us pray together in the words our Lord has given us.

Baptism is the invitation to live as a daughter or son of God. That invitation is given flesh through a life lived in union with God and in solidarity with others, especially the poor and the marginalized. Our baptism is affirmed with the fullness of the Holy Spirit in the sacrament of confirmation and is nourished and sustained through the eucharist.

The Sunday eucharist is the gathering of the community and is the time for the celebration of who we are as a people dedicated to God. For this reason, we may celebrate the baptism of infants during the Sunday eucharist, when we remember Jesus' resurrection from death to new life and are nourished by the sharing of our lives and the breaking of the bread. Each time we gather for eucharist, we remember what Jesus taught us through the stories of faith recounted in the scriptures. We ponder those stories and their meaning in our lives for this time and this place, and we hope that these same stories will shape the life of the newly baptized.

The life of the church continues in the life of each baptized person in the sharing of the story. It is nourished in the breaking of the bread and is given flesh in service for others through witness and commitment. Let us be a people who proclaim through our everyday lives that we have received the fullness of God's Spirit and that we continue to share the banquet of Christ's sacrifice!

Text by Jane Marie Osterholt, SP. Art by Laura Montenegro. Copyright 1996, Archdiocese of Chicago: Liturgy Training Publications, 1800 North Hermitage Avenue, Chicago IL 60622-1101. All rights reserved.

STUDY
GUIDE

New Life: A Parish Celebrates Infant Baptism

Timothy Fitzgerald

New Life: A Parish Celebrates Infant Baptism is a documentary of baptism as it is celebrated at Sunday eucharist in Christ the King Catholic Community in Las Vegas. This video shows the regular Sunday Masses that were celebrated on July 8 and 9, 1995, the Fourteenth Sunday in Ordinary Time. The liturgies were not staged for television; they are what this parish does each week. The core of the program is the rite of baptism; therefore the entire Mass is not shown. We see the greeting of the family at the door, the liturgy of the word, the renewal of baptismal promises, the full immersion in the baptismal waters, the sealing of the newly baptized with oil, the giving of the white garment and the candle, and the final blessing. We hear members of the parish express their support for the families, promising to nourish these newly baptized in a church that takes seriously its liturgy and its work for social justice. We come away knowing why the children and adults of this parish look forward to the baptisms at Sunday Mass.

Audiences for This Video

Whether baptism is celebrated at the Sunday eucharist or at
a separate assembly, this video is useful for parish staff, baptism
preparation teams, catechists and the parents of children to be
baptized. Religious educators, liturgy board and planning committee
members, renovation and building committee members, and teen
and adult members of parishes can benefit from watching this video.
All ministers — presiders, deacons, readers, ushers, eucharistic
ministers, acolytes, musicians — can gain insight by watching with a
special focus on their ministry within the sacrament of baptism.

Preparation

Before facilitating the video session, preview the video. Watch it
several times to familiarize yourself with the content. On the second
or third viewing, set the video counter at 00 and make note of the
counter number at particular segments that you may wish to cue up
later for the viewers. In order to facilitate the group discussion, select
from the following questions those appropriate for the viewers. To
complete your preparation, you may wish to consult the references
to the *Rite of Baptism for Children* in the discussion questions.

General Questions

1. How have the images, sounds and actions in the video spoken
to you?

> **What comments by the people do you remember?**
>
> **How did the liturgy as shown in this video
> inspire you?**
>
> **What did this video help you to understand
> about baptism?**

2. Recall to your mind and heart your own baptism.

> **When did it occur?**

Where was it celebrated?

Who was the minister of baptism?

Who else was present? Parents? Other family members? Friends? Godparents?

What would have motivated them to "bring you to baptism"?

What would have been in their minds and hearts?

How has your life been affected by your baptism?

What have been the consequences of that event?

3. In the video, the people use many images to explain and describe baptism and its meaning. Their images include "beginning of a journey," "recommitment of our vows into the community," "it calls us to the (eucharistic) table," "calls us to be one with each other." They talk about baptism as "new life," "sharing in the death and resurrection of Christ," "belonging to the community." Many of these images are used in the *Rite of Baptism for Children*.

Our Catholic tradition provides even more images to describe baptism: the font as the womb of Mother Church, our release from original sin, birth into Christ, the coming of the Spirit to the followers of Christ, the new Pentecost, an echo of Jesus' own baptism.

What other images or language would you use to describe baptism and its meaning?

Which images are most helpful to you? Why?

Questions for Parish Staff and Baptism Preparation and Catechetical Teams

1. The *Rite of Baptism for Children* expects the parish community to attend to hospitality and outreach as part of the preparation for sacramental celebrations.

What is the spirit of hospitality like within the liturgy shown in the video?

How do the parish and the priest express hospitality as part of the liturgy?

What kind of hospitality needs to exist in the life of a parish for a spirit of hospitality to be obvious within the liturgy?

If a parish liturgy is to convey a spirit of hospitality, what needs to happen in advance?

Why is such a spirit important to the liturgy?

What is the spirit of hospitality like in your parish?

How does that affect the liturgical life of your parish?

How do parishioners extend hospitality?

How do the priests and other ministers in the liturgy extend hospitality?

Who is primarily responsible for this spirit of hospitality in the parish? In the parish's liturgy?

2. The video shows that this parish and pastor have adjusted the rite. In some ways they embellish the rite (e.g., adding a procession with the pastor presenting the newly baptized to the assembly). In other ways they diminish or simplify the rite (e.g., laying hands on the child instead of anointing with the oil of catechumens; recasting the blessing prayer over the water).

How do these adjustments compare to the rite itself?

What adjustments or adaptations are appropriate to the rite and enhance the celebration of the rite?

What adjustments are inappropriate or seem not to enhance the celebration?

How do you adapt or adjust the rite in your parish?

How do you embellish the rite? How do you diminish or simplify the rite? Why?

What is the basis for doing so?

3. The rite builds upon several processions: from the door (welcoming) to the ambo (hearing the word); from the ambo to the font (baptizing); from the font to the assembly and to the altar (doing the eucharistic prayer and sharing the eucharist); from the assembly and altar to departure (to the world as the body of Christ). In this video the processions are adjusted because of the worship space and the seating arrangement.

How effective is their adaptation of the processions in the rite?

How do you adapt or adjust the rite to accommodate your worship space?

How does the video support your adaptation of processions in the rite?

How does the video challenge your pastoral practice?

4. The pastor discusses ways in which he draws upon the baptism throughout the liturgy: "I find it important to include mention of the baptism throughout the Mass beyond the times that are part of the ritual. . . . During the eucharistic prayer, I always mention the child being baptized. During the homily, I often reflect on how the word . . . applies to the child about to be baptized. At the closing, we bring the families [forward] and bless and dismiss them and encourage our parishioners to come to the child . . . and meet the family."

What are other ways the rite provides for incorporating the baptism and the family into the Sunday Mass?

What are other ways you adapt the rite to do this?

5. In the revised rite we read that through baptism and the signing with the gift of the Spirit in confirmation, the newly baptized come to the table of the eucharist. "Thus the three sacraments of Christian initiation closely combine to bring the faithful to the full stature of Christ to enable them to carry out the mission of the entire people of God" (*General Introduction to Christian Initiation*, 2).

> **What do you think of this parish's insistence that baptism be celebrated at Sunday Mass?**
>
> **Besides the obvious reason — this is the largest gathering of the parish — why do they always want baptism celebrated at Sunday Mass?**
>
> **Why does the rite itself suggest this as a practice?**
>
> **Why does the rite insist that baptism and eucharist are to be closely associated?**
>
> **When does your parish celebrate baptism at Mass?**
>
> **What are your reasons for this?**

6. Other obvious reasons for celebrating baptism at Sunday Mass spring from the church's teaching about initiation: that the community of faith itself is the central minister of initiation and reaffirms its own baptismal life when initiating others.

> The people of God, as represented by the local church, should understand and show by their concern that the initiation of adults is the responsibility of all the baptized. (*Rite of Christian Initiation of Adults*, 9)
>
> The faith . . . is not the private possession of the individual family, but it is the common treasure of the whole church of Christ. (*Rite of Baptism for Children*, 4)

> How does celebrating baptism at Sunday Mass, when this central minister is gathered, express these teachings?

> Does the regular experience of baptism help the parish's understanding?

> How does your parish learn and experience these church teachings?

7. If baptism is celebrated outside Mass, the presence and hospitality of the parish community is still essential.

> How do you arrange for the community's presence and ministry at separate liturgies of baptism in your parish?

> How do you arrange for the other ministries (musicians, readers, acolytes) that baptism always requires?

> How do you provide for the liturgy of the word, the processions and the clear relationship to the eucharist that the rite requires?

> In what ways do these smaller celebrations of baptism need to be expanded or enriched?

8. In the video, the celebration leads back to the altar, anticipating the time when the child will come to the eucharistic table. The rite expects this to be the usual practice. "After the celebrant speaks of the future reception of the eucharist by the baptized children . . . , the Lord's Prayer is recited before the altar" (*Rite of Baptism for Children,* 19).

> How does the celebration of baptism in your parish express that connection between baptism and the eucharist?

> How does the practice of Christ the King Community affirm your own practice?

In what ways does it challenge your own parish's practice?

How would you improve their celebration of baptism?

How would you learn from their celebration of baptism?

9. A member of the baptismal preparation team says that often people return to the church at the time of the baptism of a child.

What has been the experience in your parish?

How might a parish welcome these people, catechize them and heal past hurts?

Questions for Parents

1. The video highlights a parish celebrating baptism as a public experience with the entire assembly taking full part. Over a period of time, the pastor says, the parish has grown accustomed to baptism at Sunday Mass.

What do you think of this parish practice?

What are the benefits or advantages of this celebration?

What are the disadvantages or difficulties of this celebration?

How do you think such a celebration affects those taking part?

Is this different from your parish's celebration of baptism?

What are the benefits or advantages of your parish's celebration?

What are the disadvantages or difficulties?

2. The priest, parents and godparents mark the children to be baptized with the sign of the cross. This is the first time the child is publicly marked with this sign of our faith.

> **Who traced you with the sign of the cross at your baptism?**
>
> **Who first taught you the words we use with this sign?**
>
> **Who taught you to make this sign by yourself?**
>
> **Who taught you the significance of this sign we use?**
>
> **How often do you make use of this sign?**
>
> **How do you teach this sign of faith to your children?**

3. In the video, the babies are naked as they are taken into the water. What is the significance of this?

A priest commented that, having experienced this way of baptizing children, it makes better sense. A mother said it seems more honest, more indicative of standing before God in honesty. What is its significance for you?

4. The rite encourages the families to bring the baptismal garment to the church to clothe the child after baptism.

> **Do you have a baptismal garment?**
>
> **What is its history?**
>
> **Have you told the story of this garment to the children and other members of your household?**

5. Those gathered for baptism — whether at Sunday Mass or at another time — join in the Lord's Prayer in anticipation of the children eventually sharing the eucharist with the parish.

> **When did you first learn the Lord's Prayer, this prayer we always use when we gather for eucharist?**
>
> **Who taught it to you?**
>
> **When do you teach this to your own child(ren)**

About the Authors

Paul Covino is assistant chaplain and director of liturgy at College of the Holy Cross, Worcester, Massachusetts. He has written on infant baptism for *Liturgy 90, Today's Parish* and *The New Dictionary of Sacramental Worship.*

Catherine Dooley, OP, teaches in the School of Religious Studies at Catholic University of America in Washington, D.C. She is a frequent speaker and author in the areas of catechesis and the initiation of children.

Timothy Fitzgerald is a priest of the diocese of Des Moines, Iowa. He has served in parish ministry and adult education, and he writes regularly on issues of pastoral liturgy. He is associate director of the Notre Dame Center for Pastoral Liturgy at the University of Notre Dame.

Linda Gaupin, CDP, is director of the Office of Religious Education for the diocese of Orlando, Florida. A former associate director of the office of the U.S. Bishops' Committee on the Liturgy, she is a frequent author and speaker on issues of catechesis and liturgy.

James W. Moudry is the executive director of the Institute for the Christian Initiation of Children and a consultant for liturgy and sacramental practice. He taught theology and liturgy for 25 years at St. Paul Seminary School of Divinity of the University of St. Thomas in St. Paul, Minnesota.

James S. Musumeci is ordained for the diocese of Brooklyn, New York; he developed the baptism program when he was the parochial vicar of St. Laurence parish in Brooklyn. He currently serves as director of the Office of Pastoral Care of the Sick for his diocese. Jim approaches ministry with a background in human resources and adult education training.

Jane Marie Osterholt, SP, is associate director of the Office of Religious Education for the diocese of Joliet, Illinois.

David Philippart worked in parishes in New York state and Michigan before becoming an editor at Liturgy Training Publications. He is the editor of *Liturgy 90* and *Environment & Art Letter* and a frequent writer and speaker on liturgy.

Mary Alice Roth, Angie Fagarason and **Deanne Tumpich** minister at St. Julie Billiart parish in Tinley Park, Illinois, which is in the archdiocese of Chicago. Angie is coordinator of liturgy, and Mary Alice is the assistant coordinator. Deanne is director of music.

Patricia Hawkins Vaillancourt is associate director for catechesis with the family in the Catechetical Office of the archdiocese of Newark, New Jersey.